Teaching World Languages with the Five Senses

With this fun, practical guide, you will have everything you need to re-envision and reinvigorate your world language classroom. Author Elizabeth Porter draws on a brain-based approach to show how language learning is a sensory experience. Students can effectively learn languages and improve retention through activities and lessons that incorporate the five senses – sight, hearing, taste, touch, and smell. Chapters include real-world, research-backed examples and classroom strategies and activities ready for use. An essential resource for world language teachers, this book introduces language learning philosophy and an out-of-the-box, effective approach that uses neuroscience combined with best practices to promote a highly engaging language learning environment.

Elizabeth Porter is a French teacher, Curriculum Specialist, and founder of Language with the Five Senses Education. She currently teaches American Literature and US and World History in the dual-language program at the French overseas school in Dakar.

Other Eye On Education Books
Available from Routledge
(www.routledge.com/eyeoneducation)

The Ultimate Guide to Selling Your Original World Language Resources:
How to Open, Fill, and Grow a Successful Online Curriculum Store
Erin E. H. Austin

Sparking Creativity in the World Language Classroom:
Strategies and Ideas to Build Your Students' Language Skills
Deborah Blaz and Tom Alsop

The World Language Teacher's Guide to Active Learning:
Strategies and Activities for Increasing Student Engagement, 3rd Edition
Deborah Blaz

The Antiracist World Language Classroom
Krishauna Hines-Gaither and Cécile Accilien

Your World Language Classroom: Strategies for In-Person
and Digital Instruction
Rachelle Dené Poth

Enlivening Instruction with Drama and Improv: A Guide for Second
Language and World Language Teachers
Melisa Cahnmann-Taylor and Kathleen R. McGovern

Leading Your Language Program: Strategies for Design and Supervision,
Even If You Don't Speak the Language
Catherine Ritz

Differentiated Assessment for Middle and High School Classrooms
Deborah Blaz

Activities, Games, and Assessment Strategies for the World Language
Classroom, 2nd Edition
Amy Buttner Zimmer

Teaching World Languages with the Five Senses

Practical Strategies and Ideas for Hands-On Learning

Elizabeth Porter

Routledge
Taylor & Francis Group
NEW YORK AND LONDON

Designed cover image: © Getty Images

First published 2024
by Routledge
605 Third Avenue, New York, NY 10158

and by Routledge
4 Park Square, Milton Park, Abingdon, Oxon, OX14 4RN

Routledge is an imprint of the Taylor & Francis Group, an informa business

© 2024 Taylor & Francis

The right of Elizabeth Porter to be identified as author of this work has been asserted in accordance with sections 77 and 78 of the Copyright, Designs and Patents Act 1988.

All rights reserved. No part of this book may be reprinted or reproduced or utilised in any form or by any electronic, mechanical, or other means, now known or hereafter invented, including photocopying and recording, or in any information storage or retrieval system, without permission in writing from the publishers.

Trademark notice: Product or corporate names may be trademarks or registered trademarks, and are used only for identification and explanation without intent to infringe.

ISBN: 9781032275888 (hbk)
ISBN: 9781032265759 (pbk)
ISBN: 9781003293439 (ebk)

DOI: 10.4324/9781003293439

Typeset in Palatino
by codeMantra

Daniel and Noah – Both of you are my world and I love you both with all my heart. The two of you inspire me daily, and it has been amazing watching your language journeys since moving to Senegal.

May you always and forever embrace love, happiness, and adventure.

You are in my soul forever, my forever loves, the two halves of my heart.

Mom – I love you. Thank you for giving me an education, something that not everyone has the privilege of having. Thank you for allowing me to follow my dreams and my love of language far and wide. I am so grateful.

Auntie Teri – Thank you for supporting me through thick and thin and being there for me always and especially when I made the crazy decision to move to Senegal!

Iba – Sama jant- danuy tabax adduna bi ci lëkkëloo. Dama laa bëg. Amoo moroom. Jàmm rek. Danga rafet xol. Jërëjëf.

Lika – sama xarit, sama mag bu jigéen, sama khol. Man dama bëg yow. Sans toi, je ne survivrais jamais au Sénégal ! Tu m'apprends beaucoup de choses et je suis reconnaissante. C'est toujours la fête chez Elizabeth ! Keur Elizabeth mo neex ! GROS bisous!

Esmeralda – mi mejor amiga. Te amo. Me ayudaste en uno de los momentos más difíciles de mi vida. Me mostraste cómo hacer cosas difíciles. Te estoy muy agradecido. You are my best friend forever, keep being an amazing champion for bilingual education, for kids, and the amazing educator that you are! Keep fighting for equity in education. We need more teachers in the world like you!

Tara – You were my introduction to Senegal. I will miss you forever. Rest in peace dear friend.

Contents

	Meet the Author	viii
	Wolof Materials Disclaimer	ix
1	Introduction	1
2	Language Learning in the Brain	5
3	What Is Language with the Five Senses?	14
4	Culturally Responsive 21st-Century World Language Classrooms	35
5	Decolonizing the World Language Curriculum	56
6	Pathways to Fluency	62
7	Pathways to Biliteracy	74
8	Bringing the World into Your Classroom	82
9	Creativity in the World Language Classroom	100
	Bibliography	107

# Meet the Author

Elizabeth Porter is from Seattle, Washington. She is an educator with over 20 years of classroom and education administration experience. She began her teaching career in Caen, France, then taught in a dual-language elementary program in one of the French overseas schools in Seattle before becoming a high school French teacher. Elizabeth then moved into education administration, working as a curriculum specialist and instructional coach, and school principal. In 2020, she started her non-profit education organization Language with the Five Senses Education with the goal of promoting professional development programs for American teachers in the Global South as well as studying education systems worldwide to promote 21st-Century Education skills and advocate for equity in education. Elizabeth decided to return to the classroom in 2023 and currently teaches American Literature and US and World History in the dual-language program at the French overseas school in Dakar. Elizabeth has two sons, Daniel and Noah. Elizabeth lives in Dakar, Senegal, with her son Noah and her two dogs, a beagle named Oscar and a Maltichon named Snowball. You can follow Elizabeth on LinkedIn https://www.linkedin.com/in/elizabethporter1980/.

Wolof Materials Disclaimer

I am a Wolof learner and wanted to include materials that were created to help myself and other expats in Senegal who are learning Wolof the LW5S way. Because Wolof was not codified until the 1970s, there is not a consistent way people spell words. In the Wolof materials, if you are a Wolof speaker, you may see discrepancies or mistakes. I had three native Wolof speakers check the materials before including them in the book, but again, it is a language that is mostly oral and written Wolof tends to be inconsistent. If you are a native Wolof speaker, please forgive any inconsistencies or mistakes you may find in my materials and feel free to help me correct them by e-mailing me at elizabeth@lw5seducation.com.

# Introduction

Welcome to Teaching Language with the Five Senses! In this book, you'll find a wealth of tools to engage the senses and inspire teachers and students alike. Teaching languages can be challenging, but here you will find useful tips, tricks, and tools to reinvigorate your practices.

My Story

I am starting this book with a story about my son because it illustrates how I came to understand using the senses in learning another language and was the catalyst for my understanding of language in the brain. My oldest son Daniel was diagnosed with high-functioning autism spectrum disorder in 2011 at three. My family and I had suspected from birth that his brain was wired a little differently. When he was officially diagnosed, I felt a mix of emotions, from shock and numbness to gratitude and relief to have an explanation. I am the type of person, who receives heavy news, "freaks out" for about a day, and then jumps into action. With the diagnosis of autism, I had to grieve that I would not be raising a "neurotypical" child and adjust my expectations accordingly. I am an educator and believe firmly in the adage "knowledge is power," so I began extensive research on the brain. I wanted to know how I could best understand my child and best advocate for him because I knew that once he entered school, we would have incredible challenges ahead.

Introduction

When Daniel turned three and was still barely speaking, I was highly interested in why his brain was not allowing him to produce language. He began speech therapy, and we started using a communication system called Picture Exchange Communication System or PECS. PECS is a system that pairs pictures with words to aid in both receptive language comprehension and expressive language before spontaneous expression comes naturally. As I watched Daniel work with the speech therapists and we worked with the PECS, Daniel's language began to emerge, and a lightbulb went off in my head! I wondered why we do not teach using the same tools in the World Language classroom! So I went to work researching language acquisition in the brain, comparing neurotypical children to children with autism. This experience with watching my autistic son learn to communicate, paired with my experience of having a special needs child in the public education system and my love of connecting with all humans, led to the birth of the Language with the Five Senses method.

 ## Structure of the Book

Each chapter of the book will be written with the following easy-to-access structure:

- **A quote (or quotes) related to the chapter's content** – to inspire you and help you understand the chapter's content.
- **A short story** from my own teaching experience to help you explain the ideas in the chapter. The human brain is wired for stories, so telling stories will help engage you and help you retain the information.
- **Information backed up by research** – an explanation of the research because this method is backed by neuroscience.
- **Application in the classroom** – practical ideas that you can use right now in your classroom. This section also includes adaptations for in-person and alternative learning environments (such as virtual learning), suggested digital learning platforms, adaptation for different proficiency levels, and ideas for differentiation. This

section will also let you know which part of the Language with the Five Senses sequence the activity aligns.

Chapter 2 – Language Learning in the Brain

This chapter is an explanation and exploration of language learning in the brain – specifically, how the brain acquires language through the senses. It describes evidence from neuroscience to support the explanations. It also addresses how growth mindset and SMART – Specific, Measurable, Attainable, Realistic, and Timely goals support students in second-language acquisition.

Chapter 3 – What Is Language with the Five Senses?

This chapter is an overview of the Language with the Five Senses method with suggestions about how to explain the method to your students and the practicalities of the method.

Chapter 4 – Culturally Responsive 21st-Century World Language Classrooms

This chapter is an explanation and description of a 21st-Century Education and culturally responsive practices. Readers will understand the difference between 20th- and 21st-Century Education and how to foster a culturally responsive and 21st-century classroom environment in a world language context.

Chapter 5 – Decolonizing the World Language Curriculum

This chapter focuses on ensuring that the curriculum represents all students in the classroom. That all students can see themselves in the curriculum and that the curriculum represents all the people and places where the language is spoken.

Introduction

Chapter 6 – Pathways to Fluency

Many teachers ask me how to promote fluency and encourage their students to speak. This chapter explains the difference between fluency and accuracy, why translation methods do not work, and how to encourage confidence in speaking the target language.

Chapter 7 – Pathways to Biliteracy

This chapter explains the difference between being bilingual and biliterate and practices that promote literacy in the target language.

Chapter 8 – Bringing the World into Your Classroom

This chapter gives the reader specific examples of how to expose students to different cultures that speak the target language worldwide without leaving the classroom!

Chapter 9 – Creativity in the World Language Classroom

Creativity is a 21st-century skill that is as important as numeracy and literacy. This chapter explains the importance of creativity in the World Language classroom as it connects to fluency and higher order thinking skills.

    Language with the Five Senses started with a theory and has turned into a whole method for learning! This book will give you the tools to become a Language with the Five Senses teacher!

Language Learning in the Brain

I would like to start this chapter with the following quotes from Michael Gelb, Tony Buzan, and David Sousa and Carol Ann Tomlinson because they speak to the content of the chapter: "Your brain has a capacity for learning that is virtually limitless, which makes every human a potential genius." – Michael J. Gelb; "Many think of memory as rote learning, a linear stuffing of the brain with facts, where understanding is irrelevant. When you teach it properly, with imagination and association, understanding becomes part of it." – Tony Buzan; "Research is revealing so much about how the brain learns that educators can no longer ignore the implications of these discoveries for educational practice." – David A. Sousa and Carol Ann Tomlinson.

These quotes speak to how teaching practices need to evolve to be in line with what we continue to learn about how the brain is wired for acquiring new skills, knowledge, and language.

My Experience

My mother likes to joke that when my brother and I were born, we decided to speak every language except English. I have always loved languages and connecting to other cultures. I am bilingual in French and English. I have been learning Spanish, and I am currently learning Wolof. I was raised in the United States, speaking English, and traveled frequently to France throughout childhood and moved to France to study at the end of high school. I began my teaching career in France. I moved back to the

United States in 2002 and taught in a dual-language French Immersion school in the Seattle area for four years before becoming a high school French and English Language Learner (ELL) teacher. In the years that followed, I spent a significant amount of time working in global education, traveling extensively, learning about school systems in other countries, and studying the effects of language and culture on the brain.

I fell in love with Senegal during a brief visit in June 2021. Between that first visit and June 2022, I made four more visits to Senegal. Just before returning from Senegal in July 2022, I was offered an opportunity to take over one of the dual-language schools in Dakar. I did not even need to think about it, I immediately accepted, and in August 2022, I moved my two sons and I to Dakar. My sons and I are now on our own language acquisition journeys, and we are learning a tremendous amount every single day. Even though I am in my 40s, my brain is growing by leaps and bounds through all the new experiences. In two months, my sons have made incredible progress and my younger son Noah has gone from speaking almost zero French to communicating in French and in Wolof! It is amazing what happens when a person is immersed and given significant comprehensible input.

The Building Blocks of Learning

Our brains are incredible and intricate. A baby is born with approximately 100 billion neurons or brain cells. All learning is sensory. We have specialized sensory receptors located all over the body that receive information and send it to the brain. Think back to when you were in kindergarten, learning about the five senses – those are our sensory receptors! Information comes into the brain through hearing with our ears, seeing with our eyes, touching our skin (not just our hands), smelling with our noses, and tasting with our tongues. These receptors are simply messengers. They do not interpret the information into the brain; however, they help the brain prioritize. The brain only admits about 1% of the information sent by the sensory messengers because it is the only organ in the body that does not store oxygen and nutrients and uses approximately 20% of its overall resources. This prioritization is the brain's way of conserving energy and preventing sensory overload.

When sensory input comes into the brain, it is sent to an input filtering system called the reticular activating system (RAS). The RAS is a network of neurons in the brain stem formed like a net, which I like to think is nature's way of "catching" the sensory messages like butterflies! The RAS is also not responsible for interpreting the information. Instead, it readies the brain for action, detecting changes in patterns. The RAS has the same function in all mammals to filter, prioritizing changes in the norm, which might signal danger. Once the RAS accepts the information, it is sent to the amygdala, where the data is interpreted and sent to one of the two parts of the brain. The lower part of the brain is the more "prehistoric" or "reptilian" area of the brain. It is where the amygdala is located and is known as being more automatic and reactive. The upper area of the brain is where the higher-order thinking and information retention happen. This part of the brain is called the cerebral cortex, and it is where the prefrontal cortex is located.

Learning begins at the sensory level, but all knowledge is built through a network of fibers called dendrites, which build upon each other as skills are practiced and reinforced. When a new skill is learned, it is received by the sensory receptors and sent to the brain. It is then sent through the RAS, which sends energy to the entire cerebral cortex, activating it and preparing it to work! The new information is not always accepted in the brain the first time; practice and engaging more than one sensory system are essential to learning. The new skill then grows in the form of a dendrite. As the skill is practiced, reinforced, and applied, dendrites grow close together, forming a contact point called a synapse where messages can be sent to other neurons. The synapse can send the new skill information to other neurons via neurotransmitters linking to patterns of related information already stored in the brain. Dendrites continue to grow and form new synapses when learning a new skill, creating new neurotransmitters. These are the building blocks of learning!

When skills are practiced and applied, an individual connects to previously learned skills, connecting to topic-specific dendrites that have already grown, creating an incredibly complex network of knowledge. The more dendrites that grow, the larger and stronger the synapses become, and the more neurotransmitters work to connect. A person can grow 10,000 synapses on each one of the 100 billion neurons in the brain! That is an incredible amount of learning! (Porter, 2020).

Broca's and Wernicke's Areas

Language formulation is a complex, multistage process that converts conceptual ideas into sounds and signals that others can understand. *Broca's and Wernicke's areas* are the language centers of our brain. *Broca's area* is named after the French physician Paul Broca and is located in the left cerebral hemisphere of the frontal lobe of the cerebral cortex. Broca's area is associated with the expressive competencies of language production, writing, and speaking.

Wernicke's area is named after the German physician Carl Wernicke and is located in the left cerebral hemisphere in the upper part of the temporal lobe of the cerebral cortex. Wernicke's area is associated with receptive language and language processing in the brain. Wernicke's and Broca's areas work together. Wernicke's area creates plans for meaningful speech, and Broca's area takes those plans and determines the muscle movements needed in the tongue and mouth to turn those plans into vocal language.

It is incredible how few American language teachers are taught about Broca's and Wernicke's areas during teacher preparation programs as these two areas of the brain are vital in guiding effective practices. My minor was in linguistics during undergrad, so I was fortunate to have an overview of Broca's and Wernicke's areas before beginning my career. As I dove more into studying these two areas, my teaching practices became more informed. It is my hope that after reading this book, you will also become more informed in your practices.

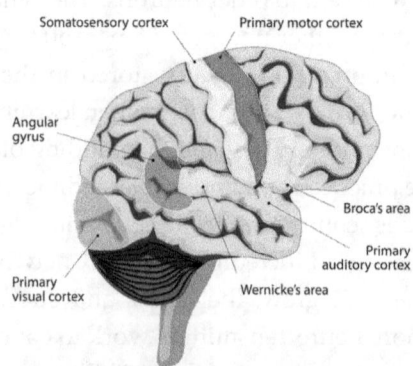

Figure 2.1 Location of Broca's and Wernicke's Areas in the Brain

Early researchers believed that different languages were segregated in the brain, meaning that a person's native language was developed in a separate area of the brain than their native language (Honigsfeld, 2019) – hence the reason language is primarily taught through translation-based methods, making the new language rely on the native language for acquisition.

However, recent Positron Emission Tomography (PET) and Magnetic Resonance Imaging (MRI) scans of the brain show that the native language and all subsequent languages share the same language system in the brain. Therefore, the native language and other languages are processed and produced in Broca's and Wernicke's areas. Yet, there were significant differences in the activity in Wernicke's area in relation to the learner's age at the time of acquisition. For example, a 1997 study found that those who learned their second language in adolescence activated Broca's area but not Wernicke's compared to learners who began studying a language before the age of 12. This finding concluded that those who start learning a second language after 12 are less likely to create language processing connections, leading to comprehension issues. On the other hand, the study also found that those who already spoke a language other than their native language could activate Broca's area even if they had passed the age of 12. Therefore, learners must begin learning languages other than their native language between birth and 12 for fluency and proficiency.

Broca's and Wernicke's areas rely on sensory input and the interaction between various sensory areas in language processing and production. For example, when a language learner sees a picture associated with a word, the visual input is transferred from the eyes through the RAS and the amygdala to the visual cortex in the occipital lobe located in the posterior part of both hemispheres of the cerebral cortex. From the occipital lobe, the information is taken to Wernicke's area for processing. It is in Wernicke's area where it becomes a phonetic representation, giving the word meaning. Finally, this representation is sent to Broca's area, where it is processed to initiate articulation. The more brain systems involved in this process, the more likely the RAS is to accept the information and send it to the correct areas of the brain and the easier it is for the language centers to process the information for language production. Further, the more brain systems involved in this process, the more likely the learner will retain the language because solid connections will be made between multiple systems. These connections between systems are essential especially in learners who are older than 12.

Throughout the book, you will find activities that engage each of the sensory systems to move new information directly through the RAS into the language centers in the brain. The examples you will find are comprised of activities that move back and forth through the steps of the Language with the Five Senses method process focusing on all four core competencies in this order: listening, speaking, reading, and writing.

Language with the Five Senses is a method that is designed to follow the natural process for language acquisition in the brain; therefore, there is always a significant focus on the receptive competencies, listening and reading, first. The method also gives students useable language they can apply immediately until their expressive competencies develop naturally. Further, I always teach students about their brains and the process of language acquisition, so they understand that the process takes time, an open mind, and lots of practice.

Application in the Classroom

This is a lesson I like to use to show students how our brains learn and, more specifically, how they are wired to acquire language.

Growth Mindset in the Language Classroom

Promoting a growth mindset in the world language classroom is critical because language learning asks students to take risks and engage in learning and experiences that are often outside of their comfort zones. The following lesson asks students to evaluate what kind of mindset they have and what it means to have a growth mindset. They then create SMART goals for the school year, helping them see that when they have the right mindset and motivation, they can do *anything*!

Figure 2.2 Brain Friendly Classrooms Activity

Book Resources QR Code

SMART goals are especially important because they allow the student to set a concrete, actionable goal. All too often, when a student is asked to set a goal, they write something down that is a bit vague or arbitrary. *SMART* stands for *Specific, Measurable, Actionable, Relevant, and Time-Bound*. In the language classroom, students will often put as their goals, "I want to speak French." That is a great goal, but it's not a *SMART* goal. SMART goals force a student to think about something very specific, ways they will know that they have achieved the goal, the specific action steps that will need to be taken to achieve the goal, that this goal will have a relevance to the class and their lives, and that it will have a deadline. Instead of "I want to learn French," a SMART goal might be "I want to learn how to order off a menu in a restaurant in French." I have students make a SMART goal at the beginning of each school year, and then we make SMART goals for each specific thematic unit. We are constantly revisiting the SMART goals and analyzing ways that students will be able to reach those goals and experience success.

The Language with the Five Senses method is based on using sensory information to connect to experiences and application of language. Asking the students to create SMART goals for their language learning allows them to connect practical skills to real-world application of the language. It also helps students realize that language learning takes time, and I find that setting specific and actionable goals lessens anxiety in students around learning and practicing the language.

The practice in setting SMART goals has been key in boosting achievement and motivation in my classroom, with my staff, and in many classrooms of teachers I have coached. In having students set SMART goals, there is an expectation that they *will* succeed; it's not even a question! When students create goals with a high expectation of success, they will put in the effort and work toward the goal. When students have the tools to do better, there is no stopping them!

3 What Is Language with the Five Senses?

I would like to start this chapter with the following quotes from Immanuel Kant, Maria Montessori, and MacIntyre and Gardner because they speak to the content of the chapter: "All our knowledge begins with the senses." – Immanuel Kant; "The senses, being the explorers of the world, open the way to knowledge." – Maria Montessori; "Language Anxiety: a feeling of tension and apprehension specifically associated with second language contexts, including speaking, listening, and learning. A good deal of research has suggested that anxiety causes cognitive interference in performing specific language learning tasks." – MacIntyre and Gardner.

These quotes set the scene for explaining how learning through the senses can help ease learning anxiety. Learning anxiety happens often in language and math classes. Learning through the senses is a way to ease anxiety by helping students use prior knowledge to build on new knowledge.

Anxiety!

Several years ago, I had a student named Leah,[1] who went on my immersion program in France. Leah had just finished her senior year in high school and was gearing up to attend Howard University as a premed student. Leah was a girl who was used to academic success coming easily to her. While she worked hard, she rarely struggled academically and had become somewhat of an academic perfectionist. There was one area, however, where she had always struggled, and that was in languages.

On the first day of immersion, students take a placement test to ensure they are in the correct classes. Leah had only attempted to study French on her own through an app on her phone. I told her not to worry. If she did not know anything on the placement test, that was ok, and she would be placed in a beginner section. Nevertheless, Leah became very anxious when the proctor asked her to put her phone away, as she was attempting to use the translator to help her get a higher score on her test. At the end of the test, she told me she was upset because she knew she did not do well. I explained to her again that it was just a placement test to make sure she was placed in the appropriate level of French.

On the second day of classes in France, I got a call from one of the school's directors asking me to come to campus to speak to a student. Leah was sitting in the main office holding her phone when I showed up, with the director standing next to her. The director explained that Leah had been kicked out of class for using her phone to translate everything the teacher was saying and for use on her assignments. Leah was visibly anxious, on the verge of tears, and claiming she was a failure.

In talking with Leah, I found out that during high school, she had a Spanish teacher who was extremely precise with language, taught through heavy translation, and got frustrated with students when they said something grammatically incorrect. I told Leah to take a deep breath, to relax, that it was only her second day in France. I also reminded her that translation would only hinder her progress and create a further block in her brain, that it was ok that she did not understand everything right away. Over the next few weeks, Leah relaxed, embraced the immersion, and ended up doing very well in the course.

Many of my immersion students express frustration that students who are the same age at the school from other countries speak French fluently, while they have taken two to three years of French and can barely say anything. This frustration on the part of students, I believe, is fostered by our collective attitude in the United States that learning a language does not matter because "everyone speaks English." I must remind students frequently that many of those students they meet on immersion, who are the same age, especially those from Europe, have taken French since kindergarten.

In my experience as an educator, I have encountered two subjects that cause extreme stress and anxiety, more than any others – math and world languages. The commonality between these two subjects is that students see them as disciplines of "absolutes." Either you are right, or you are wrong, and if you are wrong, you fail. Here is the thing with language though, it is not absolute. For many students, world language classes cause the most anxiety out of any classes they take. Surveys show that the level of stress amongst language students as "alarming." Language is how we, as human beings, interact with each other and the world around us. Language is how we get our basic needs met. Language is living and changes with generations, geographical locations, periods, and even individuals. Language cannot be considered "absolutes" because it is as complex and beautiful as humanity. Therefore, we must change our thinking about language and how we teach it.

Language Babies

In the United States, students begin learning a second language, on average, at the age of 15. Compare that to Europe, where students start learning a second language on average by the age of 6. In my experience in living in Africa, students begin speaking their ethnic language and, upon beginning school at the age of two, start learning the colonial language (French in Senegal, for example). In addition to their ethnic language and the colonial language, they usually speak one or two other ethnic languages at least at intermediate proficiency by the time they hit adolescence. Most adults in Senegal speak at least four languages.

One of the most significant challenges for American students beginning a language so late is that they expect to have immediately advanced language skills in the second language and become incredibly frustrated when they cannot understand and communicate instantly. Pair that with heavy translation methods that focus on reading and writing rather than listening and speaking. It is no wonder that 82% of Americans are monolingual compared to 19% of Europeans!

It is crucial that we, in the United States, think differently about language and the process of language learning in the brain. I always remind my students that they are French babies. Even though they may be 15 years old chronologically, the linguistic development of French in their brains is that of a newborn. *Language with the Five Senses* is a method that mimics the way we learn our native language. It helps the learner feel and experience the language fully, creating pathways in the brain that lead to language fluency.

In the first two years of study, students' language skills are as they would be from birth to two years old, no matter how old they are. They must have a solid foundation of receptive language before expressive language emerges spontaneously. *Receptive language* is the input of language, a human's ability to receive, process, and understand language in the brain. The receptive language competencies are listening and reading. *Expressive language* is the output of language, expressing needs and ideas either verbally or nonverbally. The expressive competencies are speaking and writing. Therefore, a tremendous amount of listening, repetition, and comprehensible input is needed in the early years. *Comprehensible input* is the language that learners can understand despite not understanding all the vocabulary or structures. This unconventional method is a bit of a learning curve, but students will be more likely to retain language long term.

The Language with the Five Senses method is based on five key components, which are the foundation of the educational philosophy behind the method.

1. **Performance-based** – Learners apply their learning in simulated or real-life situations. Educators in professional development use their experiences to design learning for their students that brings the world into their classrooms.
2. **Service-learning oriented** – Learners use their learning to design and carry out service projects that give back to the community and the world. Educators in professional development design performance-based thematic units based on their professional development abroad to bring the world into their classrooms.
3. **Brain-friendly** – All activities, methods, and programs are designed to grow the brain's prefrontal cortex, build executive functioning skills, and create long-lasting connections in the brain.
4. **Culturally responsive and globally focused** – Our mission is to bring the world to our learners and our learners out into the world. Educators and learners identify their own cultural identities and cultural lenses and address their own implicit biases. Thus, all pedagogy is culturally responsive and fosters critical thinking with a global perspective.

5 **Learner-centered**: Learners come first always. Relationships are the key to academic success, and every aspect of the method focuses on building solid relationships with students. The method also focuses on relationship building between learners and community members. Student learners interact with students their age to engage in cooperative learning projects across cultures.

Figure 3.1 Characteristics of LW5S Teachers and Students

What Is Language with the Five Senses?

Figure 3.1 (Continued)

Brain-Friendly – The Science of Language

The Language with the Five Senses method is a whole language and comprehensible approach that eliminates the need for translation and follows how our brains are naturally wired to acquire language. This method mimics the way the brain builds the connections to develop the native language. I cannot count the number of times I have heard, "I took two years of language in high school, and I can't say anything!" The reason for not being able to "say anything" or not remembering any of the language is twofold. First, we begin learning languages too late in the United States. While the brain can grow infinitely throughout a person's life, its language centers are the only areas of the brain that solidify and close off by the age of 12, making it significantly more challenging to learn a language past that age. Second, much of how language is taught in the United States is through translation methods and focusing on reading and writing first instead of listening and speaking.

Many second-language acquisition methods use both comprehensible input and translation, and tout that translation is proven to aid in language acquisition. Short term, this is true. Translation gives the learner the instant gratification of immediate understanding, and therefore a sense of comfort. However, long term, I have found through my research and the research of many others that translation methods can hinder fluency and retention of language in the long-term memory. Therefore, the brain will attempt to use as little energy as possible since it does not make its fuel like the other organs in the body. Thus, the brain will always default to what is familiar and ignore what it does not recognize. There are popular methods that use comprehensible input strategies, where the teacher is speaking in the *target language* or the language being learned, and at the same time writing the translation for specific words on the board. The creators of TPRS – Total Physical Response Storytelling and other similar methods swear using translation in the early years to give students understanding immediately. The problem is that the brain will immediately default to the familiar written language, and the learner will not even hear the words being spoken in the target language. Therefore, the brain *must work* to create the proper connections for language.

When teaching language, all that is easy for the brain must be eliminated, so the brain can create the connections it needs to store the new information in the long-term memory. Further, the brain cannot grow dendrites and make circuit connections unless put into a situation outside the comfort zone. Uncertainty and discomfort signal the brain to start learning because discomfort is a sensory experience. Stability and remaining in a person's comfort zone will signal the "shut off switch" for the brain. Pushing learners beyond their comfort zones is a way to eliminate anxiety and build confidence in their language skills. More details will come on how to teach without translation in the vocabulary chapter.

Another translation issue is that not everything can be translated, or it can cause cultural blunders. I have many examples from my students over the years who try to say one thing and end up saying something quite undesirable! My favorite example is the difference between *je suis excité* and *j'ai hâte*. In English, we say, "I'm excited!" for something upcoming, but in France, using the expression *je suis excité* has quite another connotation, let's just say, one that isn't appropriate for the classroom. Instead, in France, we say *j'ai hâte* to mean we are excited about an upcoming event. Another example is using the verb être ("to be") with the word *chaud* ("hot"). In English, we say, "I'm hot." In French, we say, *j'ai chaud* or "I have hot." So if you translate "I'm hot" from English to French, you say *je suis chaud*, and that is a very different kind of "hot" than the temperature! Errors between the verbs être and *avoir* are quite common in anglophone French learners but can be easily avoided if translation is eliminated.

Lastly, translation methods hinder fluency and create an environment where the learner becomes hyper-focused on accuracy. Many believe that fluency is synonymous with accuracy. However, they are not the same. I define *accuracy* as "standard book language" or speaking with 100% correct grammatical structure and precise use of vocabulary. Not even native speakers are accurate or speak "standard book language." Think of the number of Americans who do not know the difference between their, they're, and there! I define *fluency* as the speed and fluidity at which our brains can process and produce language. I further break down fluency into two categories. receptive fluency and expressive fluency. *Receptive fluency* is how much we can understand and how quickly our brains can process language received either verbally or in written form through reading. *Expressive fluency* is the speed at which our brains can process and produce language, either spontaneously or in response to receptive language.

When a person speaks, the brain follows a particular four-step process. This process is automatic when a person is speaking at a native level. The simple explanation of this process is as follows:

1. **Conceptualization** – The person thinks about what they want to say and how they want to say it.
2. **Formulation** – The person chooses the correct words to express what they want and then puts them into sentences.

3. **Articulation** – The person produces the words verbally.
4. **Self-monitoring** – The person makes sure what they have said is what they wanted to express and that the receiver of that information has understood. Then, the person adjusts the message accordingly.

Translation methods slow this process significantly because the person needs to stop and think about what they want to say and then think through the exact words they want to form in the first two stages. When the process is slowed, this can lead to frustration and anxiety by the speaker because it dramatically hinders communication. When translation is eliminated, the brain receives information through the senses and works for understanding. This process becomes automatic in the second language, just as it is in the native language. Translation is a very different skill in the brain. There is a need for translation in some instances. However, those who learn through translation methods will rarely, if ever, become fluent speakers. I have a close friend who is a translator. Her native language is French, and she translates into English, Spanish, and Portuguese. Unfortunately, the only language she speaks fluently is French. She can read and write the other languages well, but she cannot hold a conversation in those languages.

When a language learner uses the senses to derive meaning from language, translation is not needed, and the learner is more likely to retain language and skills in the brain. New forms of language, such as vocabulary and grammatical structures, become more memorable when derived from a physical experience. Therefore, movements, gestures, and physical imagery critically impact language learning, especially when a structure does not exist in the learner's first language. When the learner feels the force dynamics from which meanings are conceptualized, the language process in the brain becomes automatic in the second language. Thus, humans learn their first language precisely through physical and sensory experiences that aid the learner in permanently conceptualizing vocabulary and structures.

To clarify, "no translation" does not necessarily mean no "L1" or native language. In fact, the native language can be quite valuable in teaching culture and engaging students in meaningful discussions during the first two to three years of language study. Further, the native language is useful for helping with pronunciation through transliteration or word association. The native language can also help verify comprehension through retelling and interpretation. For example, if I ask a question in French, and the student responds to me in English but answers the question, that is not translation, showing me that the student understood. Retelling is also not translation. It is not asking a student to change words from the target language into English word for word or vice versa, or by using the same grammatical structure as they would in English, but rather explain the context of what was communicated.

Teaching without Translation

Many language teachers and learners have difficulty imagining a world where language is taught without translation, but it can be done through the Language with the Five Senses method. Language with the Five Senses uses key strategies for creating language connections in the brain that, in the long term, promote fluency and foster an environment in the brain for bilingualism. For example, the first concept taught in a first-year language class is *Clues for Understanding (CFU)*. CFU is a strategy learners can use to understand receptive language without understanding every word or structure. Further, CFU aids in expressive language during more advanced years of language study.

I give students the following on a CFU handout to keep in their notebooks on the first day of school (*see the Application in the Classroom section for the actual handout*):

1 It is essential when learning a language to focus on global meaning instead of every word. The goal for most when learning a language is to communicate effectively. You do not need to be 100% accurate to effectively communicate in another language, so the first tip is: to give yourself a break. Relax. Take a deep breath. Learning a language is a lifelong skill. Do not pressure yourself to speak fluently in a short amount of time. You will just end up getting frustrated. Instead, focus on ways to understand and try to get the "gist." When speaking, don't worry about making mistakes – EVERYONE makes mistakes, even native speakers.

2 Focus on *cognates*, or words that are similar and mean the same thing in different languages. These words are your first clue to meaning.

3. Pick out the words you know. Cognates are the first words you may recognize, but there are probably others, especially if you have been studying the language for a while. Listen or look for words that you recognize.

4. Listen or look for contextual clues. Look at pictures or listen to sounds that give you a clue to what is happening in the situation. When reading, look at the words around the word you do not understand or read the sentences around the part you are having trouble deciphering. Determine the context of what is written to help you understand the global meaning. Don't get yourself hung up on one word alone. Focus on contextual clues.

5. Listen for tone of voice and watch body language. The tone of voice can tell you quite a bit about how a person is feeling and the tone of the conversation. Watching a person's body language also gives quite a few clues to how that person is feeling in that situation.

6. Use imagines in deciphering meaning, rather than dual-language dictionaries or translators. Google Images is a great resource and will even show pictures for specific phrases.

7. Listen to music, watch movies, and read in the target language without subtitles. The more your brain engages with the language, even if you understand nothing, the more receptive your brain will be when immersed or in a more formal learning situation.

In the Application in the Classroom section, you will find an example of the first Clues for Understanding lesson I teach on the first day of language classes.

Language with the Five Senses Sequence

The method follows a set of standards and benchmarks as a guide for mastering language competencies. As you will notice, culture and global citizenship make up two of the key competencies in the Language with the Five Senses method because they give context and humanity to the study of language. In addition to the standards and benchmarks, Language with the Five Senses follows a specific sequence based on the neuroscience behind language acquisition.

1. **I Listen** – Learners simply listen to the language. They are not asked to produce at this point, only listen to the language. Listening is done through reading short stories, listening to music, watching videos, or bits of text that use the vocabulary they will learn. Production comes first through scaffolded language.
   - Students need a considerable amount of comprehensible input and listening during this time. Students will produce when they are ready, and we must not force that.
   - During this lesson stage, we simply ask to listen, repeat, and gesture words or chunks of language.
   - Teaching *lexical bundles* or *language chunks* in context helps students remember and use the language more practically.
2. **I Move My Body** – Learners are still listening. Still, now they are asked to sing the specific vocabulary words or grammar concepts while putting them together with body movements and gestures. Singing the words along with moving the body help create language connections in the brain. Singing, chanting, and body movement do two things:
   - When language is put to rhythm or music, it goes directly into long-term memory. Likewise, language is solidified when the rhythm is set to a body movement, making kinesthetic connections.
   - Singing language creates better pronunciation because we hear rhythmic language in a different way than we hear spoken language.
   - Rhythm and music promote fluency in the brain by having students receive the language and respond to it more quickly.
   - Gesture as much language as you can. Gesturing words and lexical bundles builds a language pathway in the brain that helps students retain the language.
3. **I Draw** – Learners draw pictures of the vocabulary to associate words with images instead of words with words. The teacher draws along with the students and describes the drawing while the students draw along, loading the student with receptive language and helping solidify word-to-picture associations. Drawing words also engages the kinesthetic connections.

- Drawing vocabulary words helps the students build pathways in the brain by making a kinesthetic connection to the language.
- As the students draw along with the teacher, the teacher speaks in the target language, describing each part of the picture, sometimes asking questions or having students repeat.
- If you don't feel comfortable drawing, use Google Images or clipart and describe those pictures, pointing to the different aspects.

4 **I Play** – Learners "play" with the language through very carefully scaffolded language games. When a student has fun, connections in the brain are solidified, and information goes directly to long-term memory.
- Students are more likely to retain input in the brain when they are having fun. Play games.
- Students can play games as groups or as a whole class. The more they interact with you and with each other, the more they will retain.

5 **I Create** – Students apply the language in project-based assessments that ask them to apply skills. Have students create projects that apply specific skills, for example:
- Treasure hunt at the grocery store or around town, or the school
- A cooking video
- A family photo album
- A storybook
- A poster project
- A comic strip

The possibilities are endless!

6 **I Cook** – Cooking is linguistically rich and helps the learner tap into the senses of taste and smell. In addition, cooking is an excellent listen and responds activity that incorporates culture with language.

What Is Language with the Five Senses?

In the following chapters, you will see each stage of the Language with the Five Senses sequence marked with the picture from the list to identify it quickly. Some other important tips for success when teaching the Language with the Five Senses way:

1. Do not show or write words until the "I Draw" stage, mainly first. Remember our students are language babies, and babies do not know how to read or write yet. Further, seeing the word before the students have heard and said it several times can confuse pronunciation.
2. Be animated with gestures. Speak slowly but with a tremendous amount of emotion and enunciation. I often say that as language teachers, we also must be entertainers and actors, going over the top to facilitate communication. Plus, when students find us funny, they are more likely to engage.
3. Always associate words or lexical bundles with images, not words in the native language (L1). Our brains think in pictures, and they are wired to associate language with images. Flashcards are your friends!

Application in the Classroom

Before We Begin

This activity is one I do with all my students on the first day of school to help them think about language learning. Have them look at the picture below and engage them in a discussion using the following questions as prompts:

1. Describe what you see. Don't overthink it, only the things you see.
2. How do you think this person feels? How do you know?
3. Why do you this photo might be associated with language learning? What is the message in the picture?

What Is Language with the Five Senses?

Figure 3.2 Before We Begin

Le Français Sonore

I get questions about helping students with pronunciation quite often. Many language teachers have difficulty assisting students in pronouncing words in the L2 properly, and French is especially hard. The

What Is Language with the Five Senses?

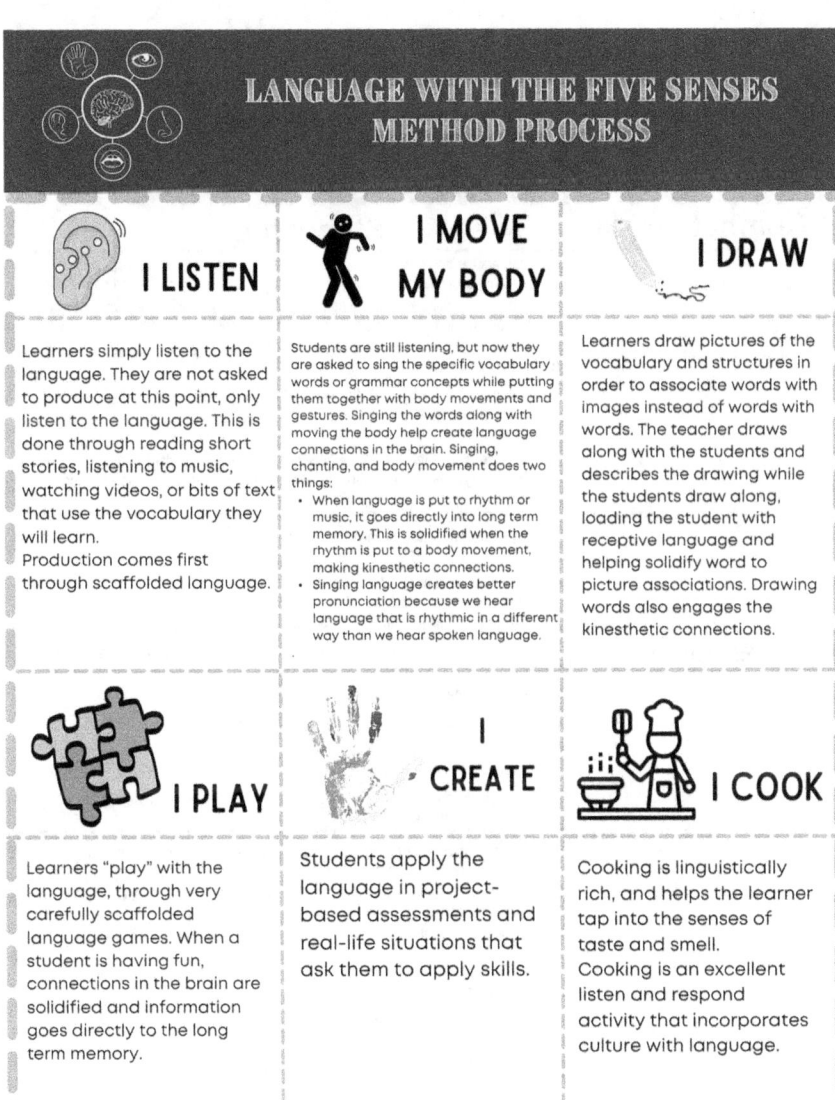

Figure 3.3 LW5S Method Process

following is an exercise I do with students of all levels throughout the year, especially in the first days of class, to help them shape their mouths to pronounce the new language. The reason why many speakers have accents is because of the way language is formed in the mouth. Those

What Is Language with the Five Senses?

LANGUAGE WITH THE FIVE SENSES STANDARDS AND BENCHMARKS FOR LANGUAGE ACQUISITION

Competencies	Standards
Communication	1.1- Learners can provide and request information, can engage in conversations in response to receptive stimulus, express feelings, emotions, opinions, and points of view. 1.2- Learners can decode written language and interpret meaning. They can discuss thoughts pertaining to written topics. 1.3- Learners can present on a variety of subjects to an audience or engage in a group discussion on a certain topic. 1.4- Learners can engage in "small talk" and respond appropriately. 1.5- Learners can communicate and comprehend with fluency in both formal and informal situations. 1.6- Learners can recognize the difference between formal, standard language, spoken familiar language, and dialectic variation and know how and when to use each linguistic variation.
Reception	2.1- Learners understand and can follow conversations in small groups. 2.2- Learners understand and can follow spoken language in larger group contexts, academic settings while watching television, videos, or movies. and in instances that are not a social setting amongst peers. 2.3- Learners can understand spoken language in everyday language. 2.4- Learners can decode, read, and comprehend written language in a variety of texts and mediums. 2.5- Learners understand and interpret body language. 2.6- Learners use **Clues for Understanding** to Interpret and understand various linguistic situations. 2.7- Learners can understand current and familiar languags. 2.8- Learners use a variety of sensory methods to help receptive language build connections in the brain.
Expression	3.1- Learners can use scaffolded, memorized expressions to initiate interactive situations or respond to receptive stimuli. 3.2- Learners can engage and participate actively in conversation using spontaneous expressive language in response to receptive stimuli. 3.3- Learners can speak with fluency and without having to stop to process language and/or translate In the brain. 3.4- Learners use **Clues for Understanding** to interpret receptive language and respond with spontaneous expressive language. 3.5- Learners can write familiar correspondence to a friend or family member. 3.6- Learners can write formal texts- essays, formal correspondence, reports.

Figure 3.4 LW5S Standards and Benchmarks

who can lose their accents in their second language have figured out how to train the muscles in the mouth and jaw to form the new language. Students get a copy of the picture below, and we practice each of the different sounds multiple times.

What Is Language with the Five Senses?

Figure 3.5 Le Français Sonore

Premiers Mots

The following is an activity I do with students to introduce *Clues for Understanding*. This exercise shows students that they can understand, even in the first week of taking French!

What Is Language with the Five Senses?

Introducing cognates and onomatopoeia is a great way to help students understand different contextual clues to help them comprehend.

Figure 3.6 Clues for Undersatnding

What Is Language with the Five Senses?

Blah Blah Blah Vocabulary

what is onomatopoeia? Can you give an example?
Did you know that the same sounds are interpreted differently because of the way different people hear language?

Let's learn how the French hear and interpret some common sounds!

la sonnette ding dong!	la réveille bip! bip!	éternuer Atchoum!	frapper à la porte toc toc!
l'eau plouf!	le klaxon tu tut!	le froid gla gla!	l'horloge tic tac!

Atchoum!

When someone sneezes in France, we say "à tes souhaits!"

Premiers Mots Vocabulary

Draw a picture for each word- no English!

une guitare 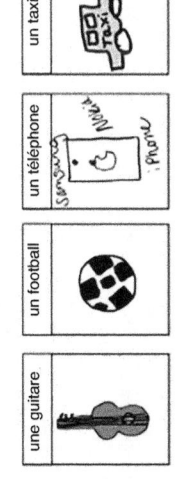	un café 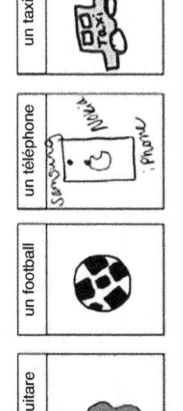	un sandwich 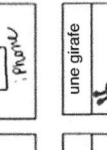	une tomate 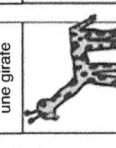
un football 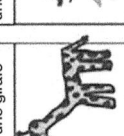	une moto 	une pizza 	
un téléphone 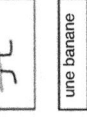	une girafe 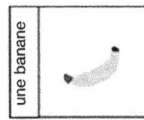	la musique 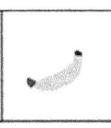	
un taxi 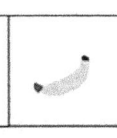	une princesse 	une banane 	

Figure 3.7 Premiers Mots Vocabulary

Note

1 Name changed to protect the student's anonymity.

Culturally Responsive 21st-Century World Language Classrooms

I would like to start this chapter with the following quotes from Nelson Mandela, Maritere Bellas, and Rita Mae Brown because they speak to the content of the chapter: "Education is the most powerful weapon which you can use to change the world." – Nelson Mandela; "Multilingualism promotes culture. A culturally diverse child is better prepared to participate and compete in a global society." – Maritere Bellas; "Language is the roadmap of a culture. It tells you where its people come from and where they are going." – Rita Mae Brown.

I chose these quotes to begin the chapter because they show that we are no longer teaching to a population of monolingual and culturally homogenous students. Our teaching practices must adapt to our changing student population. As language teachers, we are also our students' window to the world. We must emulate the cultural and linguistic diversity we want to instill in our students.

In my work with teachers worldwide, the number one complaint I hear is that more and more is expected of them without adequate support from administration and the education system itself. At almost every training I lead, there is at least one teacher that raises their hand and says, "student centered teaching through the senses is amazing, but with everything expected of me, I just don't have time to teach this way, nor do I have the support and training I need to change my practices."

While language teaching and learning has come a long way in the last century, it has not come far enough. Most American students do not begin learning a language until they are on average, 15 years old,

10 years after their European peers. Further, most students do not study a language beyond the two-year requirement for graduation.

We cannot expect our students to keep up with others around the world and participate fully in a global society without giving them proper language skills. Further, we cannot expect our teachers to serve our students if they do not have the skills or tools. Understanding the brain and how it naturally acquires language is key for moving our country forward in language education.

The Differences between a 20th-Century Education and a 21st-Century Education

Overview of a 21st-Century Education

A 21st-Century Education is an education that sets students up for success in the real world. In short, when students receive a 21st-Century Education, they are learning the skills they need to thrive in the 21st century. A 21st-Century Education means that students learn through experiences and demonstrate mastery through applying skills.

A 21st-Century Education ensures that students build their prefrontal cortex and executive functioning skills in the brain. Guiding Principles of a 21st-Century Education (in no particular order) are as follows:

- Learner-centered
- Critical thinking skills
- Problem-solving skills
- Creativity
- Communication skills
- Collaboration
- Digital literacy
- Civic responsibility
- Servant leadership
- Respect for diverse cultures

Culturally Responsive World Language Classrooms

SUPPORTING 21ST CENTURY TEACHING AND LEARNING

We cannot expect educators to provide a 21st Century Education with 20th Century practices and pedagogies. Instead, we must equip educators with an essential toolkit for teaching the skills needed to succeed in an increasingly global and technologically advanced world. The educator toolkit is the roadmap for empowering all learners. In the words of Brene Brown, "we cannot give our children what we don't have."

The differences between a 20th Century Education and a 21st Century Education:

	20th Century	21st Century
Teachers	The teacher was the expert and had all the knowledge. Teacher had the last say. Passive learning.	Teachers are life-long learners who facilitate active, experiential learning. They are partners in their students' learning.
Students	Students work in isolation within the four walls of the classroom. Students look to the teacher as expert.	Students bring a set of experiences to their education. They are the creators and producers of their own education and collaborators with their teachers, other students, and community members.
Curriculum and Instruction	Teacher centered. Focus on literacy and numeracy through rote memorization of facts. Focus on knowledge rather than an application of skills. Time-based. Low expectations. "One size fits all approach."	Real-world and performance-based. Student-centered. Outcome-based. Teachers scaffold instruction so students can apply skills and learn through experiences. High expectations. Equitable.
Discipline	Punitive and exclusionary.	Blended classroom, culturally responsive practices, relationships first. Positive behavioral supports. Maslow before Bloom.
Diversity	Diversity ignored, "everyone is treated the same" mentality. "One size fits all"	Diversity celebrated. Instruction is differentiated and equitable. Students learn about other people and cultures who are different than they are.
Technology	Print materials. Very few connected classrooms.	Connected classrooms. Globally connected classrooms. Digital literacy is crucial—paperless, digital classrooms with media and information widely available.

What 21st Century Teachers Need:
- **Positive Support and Trust from Administrators-** teachers need to feel trust and support from their administrators. They need to feel that their administrators support them and "have their backs." Classroom teachers need to feel like their administrators remember what it was like to be a classroom teacher and empathize with the challenges that classroom teachers face. Further, it is crucial that teachers feel that their administrators trust them to be the professionals they are and not "micromanage" them.
- **Respect and Trust in their Professional Abilities-** teachers are highly educated people, most of whom have at least a master's degree. All other professions are possible because of teachers, yet teachers leave the profession in droves every year due to a lack of respect and support. Teachers need to feel respected and trusted by all stakeholders and treated as professionals and experts in the field.
- **Designated Time and Resources for Ongoing Professional Development-** Teachers are often expected to engage in professional development on their own time. Yet, regular professional development is required for maintaining teaching credentials. Teachers are also often required to pay for their professional development out of their own pockets. Further, policy changes often result in teachers needing training for implementation which is usually a "one and done" affair. Teachers need designated, regularly scheduled professional development that is funded by their schools or districts. This time needs to be made part of the contracted time.

Figure 4.1 20th- vs. 21st-Century Education

- Linguistic competence – which includes bilingualism/multilingualism and biliteracy/multiliteracy
- Cultural competence
- Globally minded
- Growth mindset

- Forward thinking
- Empathy
- Responsibility to the community

Current high-stakes testing and sole focus on quantitative data to determine adequate yearly progress detriment a 21st-Century Education. By dehumanizing education and reducing students to "numbers," we have created an education that pushes math and reading. Students who are talented in other areas are not getting the chance to discover and hone those talents. The study of critical disciplines to a 21st-Century Education, such as art, music, and foreign language programs, is being cut and discouraged. This system attempts to fit every student into the same box and is not conducive to an equitable education where all students are expected to succeed.

Unfortunately, a vast majority of our current generation of students continue to be educated through the same one-size-fits-all approach as past generations, which makes little sense in the changing face of the real world. Students in our current K-12 system were born between 2003 and 2017, meaning that they have never lived without technology and the world essentially at their fingertips. These two generations, named Generation Z and Generation Alpha, are the most internationally and digitally connected in history. We must equip our teachers with the tools to teach these new generations who will never know the world without connectivity.

What 21st-Century Language Teachers Need

- **Positive Support and Trust from Administrators** – Teachers need to feel trust and support from their administrators. They need to feel that their administrators support them and "have their backs." Classroom teachers need to feel like their administrators remember what it was like to be a classroom teacher and empathize with the challenges that classroom teachers face. Further, it is crucial that teachers feel that their administrators trust them to be the professionals they are and not "micromanage" them.

- **Respect and Trust in Their Professional Abilities** – Teachers are highly educated people, most of whom have at least a master's degree. All other professions are possible because of teachers, yet teachers leave the profession in droves every year due to a lack of respect and support. Teachers need to feel respected and trusted by all stakeholders and treated as professionals and experts in the field. Administrators typically do not value or understand the importance of language programs. Language instruction is highly specialized, and there must be adequate investment in language teachers who are highly skilled.

- **Designated Time and Resources for Ongoing Professional Development** – Teachers are often expected to engage in professional development on their own time. Yet, regular professional development is required for maintaining teaching credentials. Teachers are also often required to pay for their professional development out of their own pockets. Further, policy changes often result in teachers needing training for implementation which is usually a "one-and-done" affair. Teachers need designated, regularly scheduled professional development that is funded by their schools or districts. This time needs to be made part of the contracted time.

- **Language Courses in Teacher Preparation Programs or as Part of Professional Development** – No longer are we teaching to a population of monolingual, culturally homogenous students. Our students are more diverse than ever in history and more connected than ever in history! It is no longer sufficient for teachers to speak only one language. Language learning can help teachers understand and empathize with their English Language Learner (ELL) students, but it is also proven that teachers who speak more than one language have a greater understanding of cultural diversity. Speaking more than one language ensures that our students will have success in the 21st-century real world, and we must model this for them as educators. The United States is one of the only countries in the Western world that does not require its teachers to speak another language and take language as part of their teacher preparation program.

- **International Professional Development Opportunities** – There is so much teachers can learn from teachers in other countries!

Connecting with people and places that are foreign to us helps us grow our brains and bring the world back into our classrooms. The United States is one of the only countries in the Western world that does not require an international education experience in another country as part of their teacher preparation program. Further, international collaboration experiences should be made available and accessible to teachers as a way for them to gain 21st-century skills and pass them onto their students. This is especially important for language teachers who need opportunities to maintain their language proficiency and keep up to date with new linguistic and generational cultural developments.

- **Community Advocates** – Teachers need people who are not in education in their corner. Community advocates make it possible for teachers to bring real-world learning experiences to their students. Community advocates are also essential for supporting and advocating for the work that teachers are doing to the community.

- **Education Policies That Support Data-Driven Instruction** – This means creating policies that support 21st-century pedagogies and not forcing teachers to teach to a test or focus solely on math and reading. Policies that favor standardized, "one-size-fits-all" education are failing our students. Further, all educators need to use humanized, data sources to inform instructional practices. Even more important is paying attention to the research and data that supports beginning language learning in early childhood.

- **Respite** – Teaching is a profession that requires a significant amount of giving of oneself. Teaching requires emotional investment, personal time investment, and personal financial investment. Teachers are exhausted and need a break. It is one of the few professions where a person works an entire day and then goes home and works, works on the weekends, and is required to complete professional development during school breaks. Additionally, many teachers have children of their own and responsibilities outside of school. Teachers need a rest. They need time to recharge. Their time is precious and needs to be respected.

- **Resources** – Teachers need financial support for continuing their own professional learning. They need resources they can use immediately in the classroom. They need resources in the community for extending learning opportunities outside of the classroom. They need to know how to get the resources they need to effectively serve their students. They need language instructional materials that are authentic, up to date, and culturally responsive.

Culturally Responsive Teaching for a 21st-Century Education

Cultural responsiveness is the foundation of the Language with the Five Senses education philosophy. When educators are culturally responsive, we ensure that all students are included at every step of their education journey. Cultural Responsiveness is essential for ensuring a 21st-Century Education.

LW5S Teachers

- Have the power to change the world.
- Must be equipped with a 21st-century toolkit to provide a 21st-Century Education.
- Must experience the world with all their senses and bring those experiences back to their students.
- Need support, trust, encouragement from essential stakeholders such as parents, students, school/district administrators, and the community.
- Must be treated as the expert professionals they are.

Culturally Responsive Practices and Pedagogies (or Culturally Responsive Education) refers to the combination of teaching practices, pedagogy, attitudes, instructional materials, curriculum, theories, and ideas that center around a student's culture, contexts, and identities throughout their educational career and education systems. Culturally Responsive Practices and Pedagogies disrupt the power dynamics that focus on certain dominant groups and empower students by validating their own experiences, values, and backgrounds.

Culturally Responsive Teaching is a pedagogy grounded in teachers demonstrating cultural competence and recognizing students' cultural references in all aspects of teaching.

LW5S Education Culturally Responsive Teachers

- Put relationships first, building a community amongst all members of the classroom.
- Create a climate of diversity, inclusion, and equity in their classrooms.
- Genuinely believe that all students can learn and be successful.
- See the world and bring it into their classrooms.
- Support and validate all cultural, linguistic, ethnic, and racial backgrounds of everyone in the classroom community.
- Are experienced in intercultural communication.
- Have a growth mindset and foster a growth mindset in their students.
- Use a 21st-Century Skills Toolkit for teaching 21st-Century Education.
- Understand how their own identity markers impact their teaching practices, choice in materials they use, and how they interact with students.
- Are aware of their own implicit bias and are committed to not acting from it and challenging their own thinking.
- Give students real-world experiences and evaluate through the application of skills rather than testing.
- Make learning contextual and cross-curricular.
- Encourage the safe discussion of political and social issues from all sides.

- Differentiate instruction, materials, and assessment so all students can access the information equitably.
- Nurture students' socio-emotional, mental, cultural, psychological, and physiological well-being.
- Incorporate realia and popular culture into lessons to boost relevance and student engagement.
- Demonstrate and facilitate service learning and servant leadership.
- Understand how the brain learns and use that knowledge in their instructional practices.
- Involve the outside community.
- See students as learning partners and form cognitive alliances.
- Immerse themselves in new languages and cultures with the intent to connect with others who live differently than they do as part of their own education.
- Decolonize their instructional materials and curriculum to ensure that all students have a voice.

One important lesson I have learned from working and living in Africa is to recognize differences between the white "eurocentric" culture and the "African" culture when it comes to relationship building. I have found that as a white American woman living in Africa, there are many significant cultural differences that lead to misunderstandings. I have had to make changes in my way of communicating and how much I share about myself and with students. Further, I have had to learn about the differences in the way students and teachers interact with each other here in Africa. Africans can be very suspicious of people who ask too many questions and seek too much personal information. Fostering trusting relationships in Senegal has been a different process than in the United States, and I have had to learn how to change my approach for a majority African student population. It is for this very reason that it is crucial to know your students and their backgrounds.

Figure 4.2 21st-Century Education Toolkit Characteristics of 21st-Century Educators

Book Resources QR Code

Application in the Classroom

Star of the Week

I created this star of the week activity to get to know my students and develop positive cognitive alliances with my students. This activity is culturally responsive in that I ask students to volunteer to be the star of the week. I do not force them to participate until they are ready.

This exercise is an excellent way to get to know your students and build rapport with them. Additionally, it's a good way to use comprehensible input to ask follow-up questions based on their answers and create authentic conversations. You can adapt or change these questions based on the proficiency level of your students. For example, you can ask questions that require more details or questions that require more higher-order thinking skills.

Book Resources QR Code

Figure 4.3 Star of the Week

Card Talk

Another version of the star of the week activity is Card Talk. I like to print out the card talk cards and choose one at random. Here are some sample cards with questions for each proficiency level.

Card Talk

What is Card Talk?
Card Talk is a comprehensible input activity meant to build community in the language classroom through conversation starters.

Card Talk can be used as a way to introduce thematic units, as part of a lesson, or as a filler activity for "I don't feel like planning" days. The activity can be short or last an entire class period depending on the discussion and follow up questions that result from the initial question.

Materials:
- one blank sheet of paper per student
- Pens, pencils, markers (drawing materials)
- A sample paper for yourself

Procedure:
- Ask the students a question- you can use a question from the card prompts or make up your own question. Be sure it is a question the students can easily draw.
- Say "my name is" and write your name on the board, point to yourself. Write your name on the sample paper and indicate that the students should do the same.
- Draw pictures for your answers to the question on your sample paper or on the board. Talk about what you are drawing as you draw it.
- Have students draw their own answers to the question. Make sure to tell them their drawings don't have to be perfect or anything fancy. Give them five to ten minutes to draw their answers.
- After about 5 minutes, tell the students to hold up their drawings and choose a drawing that is particularly interesting. Take it from the student and show it to the class. Have the class guess the student's answer to the question. For example, if the question is "what do you like to do?" and the student drew a guitar, you might have students guessing, "Bob likes to play guitar."
- At this point, ask the student questions like "Bob, is this true? Do you like to play guitar?" or "Do you play like Jimi Hendrix?" and even silly questions like "Are you a rockstar?" Silly questions engage the students more. Try to ask follow up questions from the 5 Ws and how like, "what are your favorite songs to play?" or "where is your favorite place to play?"
- As you ask questions to the individual student, ask the same question to the class, "Bob are you in a band? Who else here is in a band?" You can also encourage the students to ask questions based on their proficiency levels.
- Pick another card and repeat the process. Do this with three or four cards, drawing or writing details on the board as you talk with students.
- You can use these cards to create a guided story as a follow up.

Figure 4.4 Card Talk

Book Resources QR Code

Identifying Implicit Bias

It is essential in a culturally responsive language classroom that both students and teachers identify their implicit biases to create a safe and equitable learning environment. Culture and cultural identity can be charged conversations that bring up significantly strong feelings. It is important that you, as the teacher, do the work first before asking your students to do the same. Usually, I do these activities in the native language (L1) for level A1 and progressively in the target language for subsequent proficiency levels. It is important that students understand the deeper meaning in this activity, and I consider it part of teaching culture; therefore, using the L1 can be useful.

Book Resources QR Code

Identifying Implicit Bias

You will need:
- A set of stereotype cards- on the next page.
- A copy of "When We Want to Fight Bias We Can..." for each group, plus one in large poster format, projected onto a screen, or this phrase written on a large piece of butcher paper.
- 10 Post Its for each group- ideally different colors for each group

Leading the activity:
- Divide the students into groups of 3-4.
- Give each student a stereotype card.
- The students will create the life story of the person in the picture. Have them answer the following questions in their story.
  - Name this person.
  - Where does this person live?
  - What is this person's job?
  - Describe this person's family.
  - What are this person's political views?
  - Describe this person's personality and temperament.

- Have the students share the story of their person.
- Ask the students why they chose the elements of the story for this person. Lead them to understand that some of what they have chosen for this person's life comes from implicit bias.
- Ask each group to reflect on their stories and write down the elements that might come from their own implicit biases.
- Bring the students back together to discuss.
- Ask the students to brainstorm ways they can challenge their own implicit biases by asking, "how can we confront and resist our own biases? What specific steps can we take to change our viewpoints and open our minds to remove these biases?
- Have students work in their groups to create an action plan using the sheet "When we Want to Fight Bias We Can..." Give the student groups 10 Post Its.
  - Students will write their action steps for fighting bias on the Post Its.
  - Students will place the Post Its on the large chart or butcher paper.
  - Discuss each of the ideas.
- Some ideas that you can lead the students to come up with include:
  - Looking for articles that express an opposing viewpoint to gain perspective.
  - Engaging in respectful discussions with other people who may think differently.
  - Debate yourself- research the issue and present an opposing viewpoint to yourself.
  - Get to know a person who is different from you.
  - Visit another country.
  - Attend a religious service at a place of worship that is not your religion.
- Leave this poster up in the classroom or accessible to students where they can see it. Whenever the class has a discussion or an implicit bias is coming to light, refer to the poster and have the students explore the bias.

Figure 4.5 Identifying Implicit Bias

Exploring Cultural Identity

As language teachers, we are charged with helping our students discover their cultural identities in order to understand the lens through which they experience the world. The following activities are meant to help students create a profile of their cultural identities and can be used throughout the year or over multiple years (for those who have students several years in a row) to show how they have grown and changed their cultural lenses.

I also use these activities often for students traveling with me on our French immersion programs in Senegal and France. I have students do a pre-travel and a post-travel activity to show their growth both linguistically and culturally following their immersion experience.

It is essential that teachers do these activities themselves before asking students to do the same. As educators, we must do the work first. We must be examples for our students and be authentic in everything we do with them. If we have not done the work first, the students will be able to tell and will not engage as readily with the activity. Further, doing the work first helps us share parts of ourselves with our students that can help build trust.

Language and Culture Go Hand in Hand

I have always felt that language cannot be learned in a bubble, and that language and culture have to go hand in hand. Because language is such an integral part of the human existence, and human brains are wired for connection, it is essential that we have the connection to culture in order to make language relevant in the minds of our students. It goes beyond relevance though; I feel wholeheartedly that the language classroom lends a unique space to teach about people all over the world and global issues that affect the people who speak the language we are teaching worldwide.

Language teachers are in a unique position to bring up topics that might be sensitive in order to facilitate seeing things from a different perspective because oftentimes those topics directly affect people in countries where our languages are spoken! French, for example, is spoken on all five inhabited continents and amongst a highly diverse population of people. French speakers are of multiple religions and multiple ethnic backgrounds, and live in both developed and developing countries. To teach French and only focus on France and Quebec without looking at cultures in Africa, the Middle East, and Asia is doing a huge disservice to our students. It is equally important for Spanish teachers, for example, to teach about Latin America and Afro-Latinos living in the Caribbean and in Central and South Americas, rather than just Spain. Yet, as a curriculum specialist I got constant pushback when I attempted to decolonize my district's curriculum.

Language teachers do have a unique position because we are part actor, part reading teacher, part writing teacher, part history teacher, part civics teacher, part geography teacher, and all language teacher! We have to teach all the other things that go with it, culture, social justice, politics, geography, globalization, world religions, and more! All the things that make humans who they are and explain human behavior! We need to be knowledgeable about a variety of different subject areas and global issues because we are charged with bringing a unique worldview to our students! My viewpoint is that if we do not address topics that are sensitive and yet related to people who speak the languages we teach, are we really able to teach *about* those people? Are we really doing justice to the language? Language doesn't exist without humans, and humans have varying lifestyles, viewpoints, issues, and identities. How can we teach a language without teaching all facets of what it means to be a human who speaks that language?

Cooking as Culture

Cooking and eating are major sensory experiences. Cooking is also linguistically rich. Giving students the opportunity to try different foods from around the world helps them develop open-mindedness around foods, develops their palates, and taps into the senses of taste and smell through the sensory receptors in their noses and mouths.

My school happens to have a nice kitchen that all of the teachers can use to cook with their students, and we do this often here in Dakar. I used to collaborate with the foods lab teacher to create cooking experiences for students. During remote learning, the students and I would cook together over Zoom. I would cook in my kitchen and the students would do exactly what I was doing in their own kitchens.

Often, teachers ask me about equity when it comes to cooking because not all students have access to food or nice kitchens to cook in. To address the issues of equity, I will often buy recipe ingredients out of

Figure 4.6 21st-Century Education Framework for Language Teachers

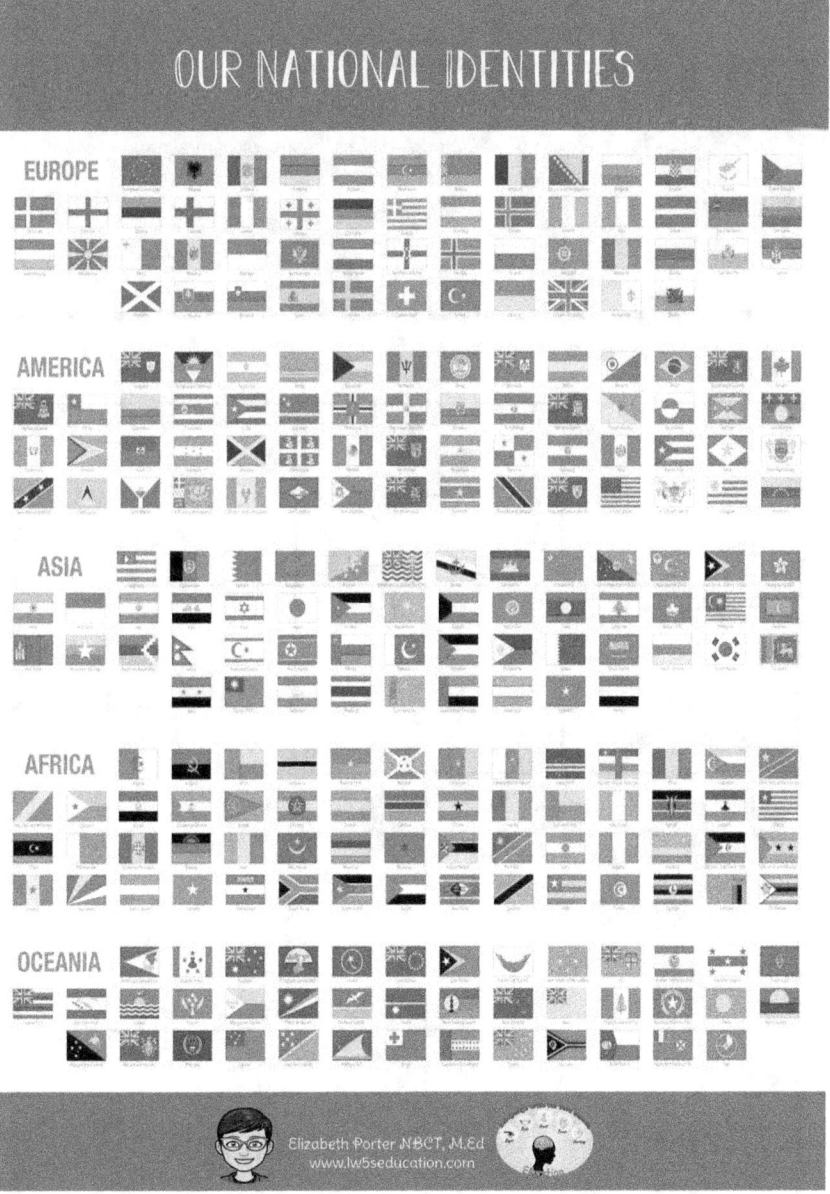

Figure 4.7 Our Personal Identities

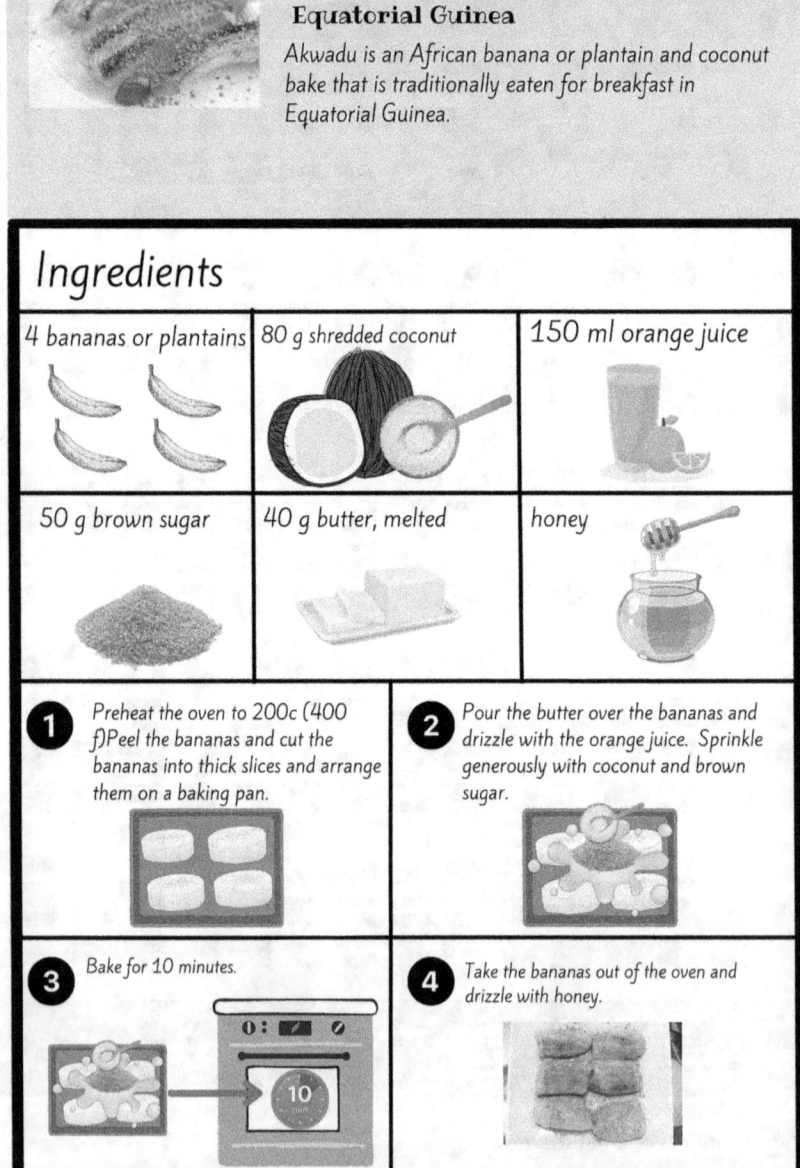

Figure 4.8 Akwadu – Recipe from Equitorial Guinea

my own pocket or use the department budget to purchase ingredients. I create as many opportunities as possible for students to cook at school. When I was a classroom teacher, and not a principal, I worked often with our lunch staff in the school's kitchen and with the foods lab teachers to allow for use of the school's cooking facilities for students both during the school day and at scheduled times after school. My French students really enjoy cooking from West Africa called Mafé. We also often make Jollof Rice here at our school in Dakar. I have also made macaroni and cheese, chili, and cheeseburgers for students to try American food in English class. Our Spanish teacher here cooks Arepas and makes recipes from Spain like Paella and a recipe from Equitorial Guinea called Akwadu from plantains.

Book Resources QR Code

5 Decolonizing the World Language Curriculum

I would like to start this chapter with the following quote from Lupita Nyong'o, Karis Clark, and Junot Diaz because they speak to the content of the chapter: "What colonialism does is cause an identity crisis about one's own culture." – Lupita Nyong'o; "By opening ourselves to knowledge systems from all over the world, we gain the critical consciousness necessary to see reality, and once we recognize reality, we recognize the necessity to deconstruct the colonial barriers that prohibit societal uplift." – Karis Clark;

> Recognizing the long histories of bias, racism, and exclusion created to perpetuate these dismal inequalities...none of this will change unless we work actively, mindfully, and collectively to dismantle the often obscure structures of power that exist both within us and without. The only thing decolonizing seeks to exclude are the forces, systems, and habits that continue to have too much power in this world and in our hearts.
>
> – Junot Díaz

I chose these quotes to begin this chapter because living in Francophone West Africa has made me even more aware of how colonization has affected indigenous and ethnic populations around the world. The people who now speak the colonial languages are those who have strong histories and their own cultures that add richness to the languages. Understanding the history of the languages we teach in the countries where they are spoken shows that we understand the people and recognize their realities. It is also crucial that our classroom environments and materials reflect all students in our populations.

I recently worked on a curriculum adoption committee for World Languages in a local school district. This was the district I lived in for nearly ten years and where my children attended school, therefore I had a vested interest in the work of this committee. At the same time, I was serving on the state World Language Advisory and World Language Standards committees for the state of Washington's Office of the Superintendent of Public Instruction.

The school district is in an area of Eastern Washington State that tends to have very conservative political perspectives and where progress in cultivating diversity, equity, and inclusion in schools is slow. This area of the state is not moving at the same pace as the West side of the state in adopting curriculum that represents all students equitably. As I worked on both committees simultaneously, the divide between the state and the district became increasingly apparent to the point that my suggestions about ensuring representation of all student populations within the pages of the textbook were met with strong arguments by parents. Unfortunately, stories like these are increasing in nature to the point where parents are passing laws to keep educators from adopting materials that represent all perspectives and cultures.

Decolonizing Education

Currently, *decolonizing* curriculum and our overall education system has been an important step in ensuring representation and validation of all students who walk through the doors of our classrooms. **Decolonizing education** refers to rebuilding the education system that supports all students, staff, and teachers by confronting the colonizing practices that continue to influence education. **Decolonizing the curriculum** brings more accurate, more inclusive, and more culturally responsive materials into the learning environment and teaches all sides of a story and all perspectives.

Decolonizing the curriculum means identifying, interrogating, and dismantling the power structures that carry a legacy of racism, imperialism, and colonialism in producing knowledge. Decolonizing the curriculum is a conscious effort to change how knowledge is produced and a commitment to contesting the assumption that white, Western, European intellectual traditions are superior and universal.

Decolonization of Education Is Critical Because Everyone Succeeds When Students of Underrepresented Populations Succeed!

A Decolonized Education Means:

- Involving students in the creation of knowledge and application of skills.
- Containing learning outcomes that address power and social justice.
- Embracing diverse linguistic backgrounds and promoting the learning of languages.
- Allowing for linguistic choice in interactions and learning tasks.
- Diversifying instructional materials to ensure student representation.
- Acting for systemic change to address the forces that damage groups of students who have been historically underrepresented and affected by racism or bias.
- Teaching history from all sides.
- Embracing the discomfort and facilitating the critical, difficult conversations.
- Fostering critical thinking.

Action Steps for Decolonizing the Education Environment:

- Educators do the work first to challenge implicit bias and preconceived ideas. Research and engage in professional learning to understand what it means to *decolonize education*.
- Implement a performance-based learning model (also known as experiential learning, project-based learning, or inquiry-based learning).
- Diversify instructional materials and content.
- Create learning outcomes that address social justice.

- Implement service learning.
- Implement assessments that allow students to demonstrate mastery in a variety of ways.
- Evaluate instructional materials and content for representation of diverse populations.

Questions for Educators to Assess Their Own Belief Systems in Education:

- What is your definition of success? What does a successful person look like? Who are some people you see as successful and why do you believe they are successful?
- What are your expectations of your students? How do they know your expectations? Do you hold the same expectations of all of your students?
- How do you create opportunities for all students to be successful according to your expectations?
- Is there a difference between equity and equality? If so, what is the difference?
- Who is speaking most of the time in your classroom? What is the ratio between teacher talk time and student talk time?
- How do you speak to your students? What language do you use? Do you know how to speak using equitable and inclusive language? Is your language equitable and inclusive?

Application in the Classroom

The following is a Curriculum Audit Framework you can use to evaluate whether the materials you are currently using or may use in the future meet the criteria of a *decolonized and culturally responsive curriculum.*

When choosing materials for use in your classroom, consider the following:

- Are the materials authentic? Where are they from? For example, if you are a French teacher, consider authentic materials that come from Francophone Africa. Authentic materials might include realia, picture books, novels, artwork, and music.

- What is the perspective of the resource? Is the perspective of the information in the resource representative of multiple perspectives or one perspective? What other resources could you use to bring in other perspectives and voices?

Diversity Equity and Inclusion		
Criteria	Meets Criteria? Y/N	Evidence
The curriculum represents individuals of diverse backgrounds, identities, and perspectives.		
The curriculum reflects historical accuracy from all perspectives, highlighting the experiences of marginalized populations with honesty.		
The curriculum represents experiences of historically underserved groups are not reduced and limited to their experiences of suffering. They are represented positively.		
Systems are in place that ensure that all learners can meaningfully participate and fully access the benefits of the curriculum without undue burden.		
The curriculum fosters joy, thriving, belonging, and liberation for all learners. The curriculum does not cause harm to any learners.		
The curriculum allows for the establishment of positive and trusting relationships, and learning partnerships between learners and teachers.		
The curriculum allows for evolving learning needs of learners.		
The curriculum uses inclusive language.		
The curriculum compares, explores, and honors home cultures.		
The curriculum provides opportunities for multiple opportunities and instructional strategies.		

Figure 5.1 Culturally Responsive Curriculum Audit

- Thinking about the specific students in your classroom, how does this material represent their voices and perspectives? Will this material help them feel validated? Will they be able to identify with the material, connect, and engage authentically with it?

6

Pathways to Fluency

I would like to start this chapter with the following quotes from David Crystal, Oliver Wendall Holmes, Wade Davis because they speak to the content of the chapter: "Fluency is the smooth, rapid, effortless use of language." – David Crystal; "Language is the blood of the soul into which thoughts run and out of which they grow." – Oliver Wendall Holmes; "Language is not just a body of vocabulary or a set of grammatical rules. Every language is an old growth forest of the mind." – Wade Davis.

These quotes introduce the concept that fluency and accuracy are not necessarily one in the same. Language the way in which we interact as humans with each other and the world around us. To speak fluently means that we speak in a way that others understand and with ease.

I am currently learning Wolof. I recently moved to Dakar, Senegal. Senegal is a Francophone country that was formerly a part of French West Africa. The official language of Senegal is French; however, a large majority of the people speak Wolof in their everyday lives. There is a famous quote from Nelson Mandela that says *"If you talk to a man in a language he understands, that goes to his head. If you talk to him in his own language, that goes to his heart."* I want to speak to the hearts of the Senegalese people by learning their language and showing them that I want to be part of their community.

Wolof is an interesting and rich language. I tried taking a Wolof class before moving to Senegal, and while I had an excellent teacher, who is also my friend, it did not stick in my brain. Within about two weeks of immersion, I was starting to understand the Wolof being spoken between my friends and colleagues. I am still in the listening phase, but I have chunks of language I can pull from when I want to try to communicate in Wolof. They key to fluency is practicing authentic language in a way that creates linguistic connections in the brain so that the brain can process receptive language and eventually produce spontaneous, expressive language.

A few years ago, I was asked to coach a French teacher who was struggling to get her students speaking. The day I came into her classroom to observe, she informed me they would be doing a speaking test, and she was going to give them 5–10 minutes to prepare. As I walked around the room, I noticed that the students had lists of questions they would be asked on the test, and they had written their responses, many of which were directly translated from English. The students had also translated the questions into English. No wonder this teacher could not get her students to speak, they were terrified of failure and being judged when speaking. That is a tremendous amount of pressure on a language learner that can cause irreparable harm!

I am not a fan of speaking tests for a couple of reasons. The first is that they cause an extreme amount of anxiety that can cause a mental block. The second reason is that, often, speaking tests do not provide a context that promotes fluency. The students were extremely anxious, trying desperately to pronounce the words on their papers and not understanding what they meant or the context without the translations. These students were not asked to use the language in a way that was authentic and communicative.

Fluency versus Accuracy

Language learners and some language teachers alike tend to confuse fluency with accuracy. There is a significant difference between *fluency* and *accuracy*. I define *fluency* as the speed and fluidity in which our brains can process and produce language. I divide *fluency* into two categories: *receptive fluency* and *expressive fluency*. *Receptive fluency* is how much we can understand and how rapidly our brains can process receptive language or what is being said to us. *Expressive fluency* is how rapidly our brains can process receptive language and produce language either spontaneously or in response to receptive language. *Accuracy*, on the other hand, is, I believe, the product of translation-based methods and creates a sense of anxiety in learners. It is the focus on each word and grammatical structure being correct. Fluent speakers of languages are not always accurate, and that is ok. When focusing on fluency rather than accuracy, we remove the anxiety that comes with attempting to communicate in the target language.

Further, these definitions of fluency refer to oral language. Written language and literacy come later as our brains process oral language first. Therefore, it is essential that as language educators, we create a toolkit of useable language that students can apply in practical situations. This linguistic toolkit includes significant *comprehensible input* and *lexical bundles* paired with exercises that build linguistic connections in the brain. *Comprehensible input* is language input that can be understood by listeners despite them not understanding all the words and structures. *Lexical bundles* are useable chunks of language taught in context that learners can use to communicate immediately.

Application in the Classroom

The Clap Snap

When words or lexical bundles are combined with gestures and rhythm, they are more likely to stick in the long-term memory, even if the gesture has no relation to the meaning of the word or bundle (Gelitz, 2021). The *Clap Snap* is an exercise where, together with the students, you clap and snap the words or structures while saying them out loud. You incrementally increase the speed of the clap snap to help the brain process and produce the language more efficiently and develop fluency. I do this with vocabulary, lexical bundles, verb conjugations, and basically any other linguistic structure I would like my students to retain. I encourage them to do the clap snap on their own to practice as well.

Vocabulary

The *Language with the Five Senses Method* (LW5S) is a brain-based language acquisition method that uses *Clues for Understanding* coupled with authentic materials and sensory experiences to promote language acquisition in the brain. *Clues for Understanding* are comprehensible and contextual clues that help language learners derive meaning from any linguistic situation. *Clues for Understanding* include cognates, images, tone of voice, sounds, smells, or words the person already understands. In addition, *Clues for Understanding* are sensory information that facilitates carrying linguistic input to the brain's language centers.

You will often see a vocabulary list included with our materials that has a word or phrase accompanied by an empty box. The vocabulary list is usually no more than 20 words or phrases.

The vocabulary list is designed in such a way that the teacher can provide as much sensory input as possible to enable the student to retain the information. Because the brain processes new information more readily in images, new vocabulary is always taught through drawing pictures of the words or phrases accompanied by body movements and rhythm. The rhythm also helps increase fluency by aiding the brain to process and produce linguistic input more readily.

Once the students have a solid understanding of the vocabulary and understand the context through *Clues for Understanding* and receptive competencies, they can move onto building their expressive competencies. Vocabulary and grammar are taught through thematic units. Each unit follows the Language with the Five Senses method process mentioned in Chapter 2.

Sample Wolof Vocabulary List

Phrases Utiles
Faites un dessin pour chaque mot de vocabulaire- pas d'anglais! Put a star next to the cognates

Nanga Def	Ba beneen yon	Ba suba	Ba leggi
Jamm nga fanaan	jerejef	Noo ko bokk	Noo tudd
___ la tudd	Ban reew nga jogge?	American la	Ñaata att nga am?
Naka was kër gi?	Dama am ben laj	Xamuma	Xammu ma limmu tekki

Figure 6.1 Sample Vocabulary Sheet for Wolof

Pathways to Fluency

French Vocabulary Unit

Figure 6.2 On Va Où Cet Été – Sample Vocab Unit

Sports in the Language Classroom

Any type of physical activity paired with language is more likely to be retained in the long-term memory. Teaching through physical activities

Pathways to Fluency

such as sports, leisure activities, and physical games is an excellent way to engage students. I love to play Pétanque with my French students, and I have been teaching my English students about baseball here in Senegal. Soccer is also an excellent sport to teach because it is very popular in most countries worldwide and fits in well with many languages.

Pétanque (pronounced paytonk), also called "boules," is one of the most popular games in France. On any given weekend afternoon, you can see French people enjoying a leisurely game. This game can be played by anyone at any time, and oftentimes you will see people of all ages playing together. The best part is that this game requires little or no special preparation. The game was invented in 1910 in a small town in the south of France called Ciotat, but a similar game has been around since ancient times.

The game is played by two opposing teams who try to throw large metal balls, called boules, as close as possible to a small wooden ball called a cochonnet. The game is played in seven rounds and each team alternates until the last ball is thrown for that round. The team that has its ball closest to the cochonnet by the end of the round, wins that round. The team that wins the best out of seven rounds is the winner of the game.

Watch the YouTube Videos about Pétanque and answer the discussion questions in your group.

- https://youtu.be/kPn4mekXYn4

- https://www.youtube.com/watch?v=YXUkofUi-ps

1. Who invented the game of Pétanque and why?
2. Who can play Pétanque?
3. What are the rules of Pétanque?
4. What are the balls called?
5. How are the balls thrown in Pétanque vs. the old Provençale game?
6. How many Pétanque clubs are there in Marseille?
7. Which French greeting did you see in the video "The French Game of Pétanque?"
8. What is the most important part of the game?
9. What matters most in this game?
10. What are your impressions of the game? Would you like to play? Why or why not?

Figure 6.3 La Pétanque

In teaching a sport, we will review the simple rules of the game and go over key vocabulary. I like to find demonstration videos also of the sport and engage students in a video talk where I describe what is happening in the video and ask the students questions about what is happening in the video. After going over the game linguistically, it is then time to play the game! I have found that even students who are not particularly athletic or into sports enjoy getting outside to play a game!

Sample Vocabulary Pages with Drawings

When teaching the vocabulary it is best to draw pictures of the words or structures, and as you are drawing, you are describing what you are drawing. Also, as you are drawing, the learners are drawing with you. All three of these components must be present to create the connections in the brain.

Figure 6.4 Sample Teacher Vocab Sheets

Chat Mats

Chat mats are a tool that is used by many language teachers to provide students with necessary vocabulary and structures to communicate specific messages. Language with the Five Senses' chat mats are simple and combine pictures with words to help learners communicate responses to specific questions. I like to use the chat mats and for Card Talk, question of the day, or sometimes I use them to help in guided writing activities (featured in the next chapter).

Figure 6.5 Sample Chat Mats

Global Classrooms
Unit 1/Unité 1

My Community and Me
Ma Communauté et Moi

Figure 6.6 Global Classrooms – My Community and Me

Book Resources QR Code

7 Pathways to Biliteracy

I would like to start this chapter with the following quotes from Johann Wolfgang Von Goethe, Frank Smith, and Junot Diaz because they speak to the content of the chapter: "Those who know nothing of foreign languages know nothing of their own." – Johann Wolfgang Von Goethe; "One language sets you in a corridor for life. Two languages open every door along the way." – Frank Smith; "You can never understand one language until you understand at least two." – Junot Díaz.

These quotes introduce us to the concept of biliteracy and the difference between bilingualism and biliteracy. They set the stage for how knowing another language helps us understand our own languages better and creates a space for expanding our worlds.

Years ago, when I taught high school French, I implemented Sustained Silent Reading at least once per week. I also read aloud to my students frequently from books I purchased in France. The books in the classroom library were authentic and based on the proficiency levels of my students. All of the books were labeled with the appropriate proficiency level, and I would often feature books that matched our current thematic units.

I remember being called into the principal's office one afternoon. The principal shared with me that a parent had called and complained that we were wasting time in class with silent reading and that I was reading books to the students that were meant for elementary children, not high schoolers. I find that often administrators have never been language teachers and do not understand linguistic education. My principal at the time was no exception, and no matter how hard I tried to explain the process of language acquisition in the brain and supported my claims about literacy in the target language with research, I got pushback.

In recent years, there has been a huge push toward biliteracy. *Biliteracy* is defined as the ability to effectively communicate or understand written thoughts and ideas through the grammatical systems, vocabularies, and written symbols of two different languages. The idea is that people who are bilingual or multilingual can transfer literacy skills across languages (Bialystok et al., 2005). Not all bilinguals are biliterate. For example, my children are bilingual in French and English, but their reading and writing skills in French are still developing. I have known several colleagues and friends who are from other countries and who speak their native languages with their children at home, but their children are only able to speak the language, not read and write. One French colleague worried about her daughter being able to read and write in French because her daughter was born in the United States and had only gone to school in English. Her daughter was bilingual, but not biliterate.

Our brains acquire languages through the same process no matter if it is our native language or 20th century language. Literacy, therefore, is as important in the second-language classroom as it is in the classroom where the native language is spoken. There is a huge push currently for "comprehensible" reading materials made specifically for Comprehensible Input (CI). My issue with "CI"-specific materials is that often they are translation heavy. I like the use of authentic story books and graded readers rather than CI books because they bring genuine culture to the learning. The key is using literature that is at the proficiency level of the students.

As I stated earlier, I think of my first- and second-year students as language babies. Therefore, I find that it is quite appropriate to use picture books that I would read to young children. We begin with regular read alouds, and weekly SSR, using Clues for Understanding to understand the story.

Book Studies

I *love* book studies. I would say that probably 80% of my thematic units that I write are book studies because they lend themselves so well to performance-based learning and cross-curricular lessons. I even use book studies as lessons within thematic units, and I would venture to guess that 99.9% of all of my thematic units, if they are not a book study themselves, have a book study integrated somewhere in them. Many think a book study is synonymous with a novel study and that, especially in a foreign language class, it can only be done with upper-level students. I'm here to tell you, you can make a high-quality book study out of any book! Novels, nonfiction, and even picture books! I made a full book study out of *Brown Bear, Brown Bear* in French (*Ours Brun Dis Moi*)! In fact, *Brown Bear, Brown Bear* is available in several languages, including Spanish and Arabic! Any picture book will work, especially one that lends well for student participation during a read-aloud. I will explain exactly how I create a book study, including how I choose books, create the activities, and integrate them into the curriculum.

We know that reading promotes language. Multiple studies have shown that young children are read to, develop language skills more quickly and have larger vocabularies than children who are not (Grabmeier, 2019). This is no different in a foreign language. I am constantly reminding my students that they are "language babies" and that even though they may be a teenager and have teenaged language skills in their native language, their brains have not developed the same skills in the new language. It is for this reason that I use a lot of picture books in the first two years of language, and then we eventually graduate to graded readers and easy novels.

Reading books in language class really helps put vocabulary and grammatical structures in context for students, exactly like when they learn their native languages. Learning through stories and the process for becoming readers is really the same whether it is a student's first language or second or fiftieth. The brain needs to listen first, put words into a context, and associate those words with images. Picture books are so important in the early years of language learning. The brain will eventually be able to create its own imagery from worse; however, that does not happen for quite a few years, just as with a person's first language. I use an *Ours Brun, Dis-Moi* study with all of my French students, elementary all the way up to high school! I have even used it with adults. I love it because it's so simple, and even in the first four weeks of learning language, the students feel successful that they could listen, understand, and accomplish a task using the language from the story! Other books I use are *La Chenille qui Fait des Trous (The Very Hungry Caterpillar which is also available in multiple languages)*, fairy tales, and other children's picture books. Whenever I am in France or another francophone country, I buy books, tons and tons of books! You should see my office; it's literally filled with French story books! We progress through stories just as you would with a child. The stories are very simple at first, and we progress until we start using graded readers, and then around the third year we do our first novel study which is usually Petit Nicolas, and we also do a unit on *les bandes dessinés* (comic books) and *Astérx et Obélix*. Fourth and fifth years are all literature based, starting with *Le Petit Prince* (The Little Prince). I love using folktales and have found several folktales in Wolof on YouTube that I have been using in my own language acquisition journey!

Honestly, by the fourth year of language study in an American high school (Porter, 2019), the students have the equivalent amount of language in their brains of about a ten-year-old child, so I don't read Camus with them. Many teachers have their high school seniors read *L'Étranger* by Camus, and while most are mature enough in English at that age to read it, I don't feel like adult literature is where the students are linguistically at that point in their studies. L'Étranger is easy enough to read, but I still think it is slightly too complex for a student who has only really gotten 480 hours of language *at most* in their high school language studies. That's not even half of the number of hours they need at their age to acquire true fluency. They still have several years ahead of them before they will be to where the brain accepts the nuances in books like *L'Étranger*. So in fourth- and fifth-year French, I typically stick to books like *Arsène Lupin, Le Petit Prince, Le Compte de Monte-Cristo*, and *Vingt Mille Lieues Sous les Mers*. Occasionally I pull out books like *Harry Potter* and *The Hunger Games*, because they are popular, and the kids like them. I feel that the use of book studies in the world language classroom is essential. Reading books translated from English that the students already know is very useful because they already have a connection to those stories.

Book studies bring a richness to the curriculum and a different perspective, and are easily cross-curricular. When a curriculum is designed around and/or heavily integrates book studies, it's amazing the thinking that happens on the part of the student!

Guided Writing

I love Guided Writing because it's a great way to boost writing proficiency and holistically teach grammar. The best part about Guided Writing is that it can be adapted to any proficiency level and any topic. Guided Writing can be done as a planned lesson or as a filler activity on the fly. Guided Writing is highly adaptable, which is why it is highly impactful. *Guided Writing* is an activity in which the teacher and the learners write together. The teacher facilitates the writing through asking probing questions that are comprehensible to the students.

Many teachers who are getting started with Guided Writing like to create an example text before doing the activity with students, especially when writing a nonfiction text. Usually, when creating an example text, I write out the details I feel are essential, and then I highlight specific words or phrases I want the students to "fill in." I lead them to these words and phrases by asking them comprehensible questions.

Guided Writing is a very useful tool in the language classroom because it can be adapted to many different types of writing, and there are multiple ways the activity can be extended. I use guided writing regularly. In the Application in the Classroom section, you will find several examples of Guided Writing activities along with extensions and student work samples. Further, in the following chapters, you will also find examples of Guided Writing activities embedded in the samples provided.

Application in the Classroom

Book Studies

Brown Bear, Brown Bear

I have two different book studies for *Ours Brun Dis Moi/Brown Bear, Brown Bear*. The first is made up entirely of images, teaching students how to retell the story in the target language. The second asks them to create their own stories based on the linguistic pattern of *Brown Bear, Brown Bear*. I have used both lessons together for a linguistically rich learning experience.

Silly Character Stories

Silly Character Stories is an activity that is incredibly easy to do on the fly with zero planning. Depending on how much you scaffold it, it can be adapted to different proficiency levels and specific vocabulary and grammar concepts. The activity essentially guides the class to create a silly character and then write a short story about that character. Once the story is written, the class reads it together in choral reading, and then the students illustrate the full story on their own.

To begin, each student will need a blank sheet of paper, a pencil, and some markers, crayons, or colored pencils. In addition, you will need whiteboard space and markers, or when I am in my own space, I like to use my easel and large Post-it papers. I like to use the easel because I can move it around the room so students can see better. I also like to write stories on the Post-it papers because I can keep them. If you are using the Post-it papers, a good set of poster markers is also essential.

To Begin, I Remind the Students of the Rules of the Activity:

1 **No translating** – Remember *Language with the Five Senses* is a zero-translation method. That means I tell students not to translate what I am saying. In the first year and sometimes second, they will shout things out at me in English because they don't have the word for it in French, and I will say it back to them in French. Technically this is translating, but I like to encourage their ideas, and when I write it on the board, I draw a picture of it. I let this slide usually but see rule number two for how I mitigate this issue further. If I hear a student shouting something out that I have said in English, I say, "NO NO! *Pas d'anglais!*" (NO NO! NO ENGLISH!).

2 **If you don't know the word for something, you can draw it, describe it, or find a picture of it** – Instead of defaulting to English, I encourage students to communicate their ideas in different ways. For example, they can do a Google image search of the picture (most students have devices these days), they can draw a picture of it, or they can describe it.

3 **Don't draw anything until I say "DESSINEZ!"** – Students often get really excited to draw, but I want to have them listen first to all

the directions before they draw. They must listen for "*dessinez*" and then the directions. I also tell them not to add any color to their drawing until the class has decided on the color or colors. Only draw what I tell them to draw and that follows the word *dessinez*.

To begin, I ask for students to name random "things" that we could make into silly characters. It could be anything. In the video, we had a book, a computer, a squirrel, and a monkey. In other classes, we had bread, toast, a chicken, and a sweatshirt. I write these ideas on the board and draw a picture (badly, I left my drawing skills in kindergarten) to go along with them. I then ask the students to vote on which "thing" they want to use to create a character.

The next step of the activity is to ask students questions about the character. My first question is about the character's size – is it a tiny monkey, a normal-sized monkey, or an enormous monkey? Students vote on the character's size and then I say, "ok *classe*! *Dessinez un singe énorme*!" The students then draw an enormous monkey on their paper (or whatever they decide is the character and the size). Nothing else is drawn yet. I continue the activity by asking them to imagine the character and asking them leading questions about the character such as:

4. **What color is the character?** – I write all the colors the students shout at me on the board and then ask if the character is one color or all the colors. If they say one color, we vote on which color they want and then color the character that color. If it is all the colors, I tell them to color their character all the colors.

5. **What is the character wearing**? – Again, I write down their answers, and we vote on what the character is wearing. Elicit as much input as possible, what color are the clothes, are they too big or too small for the character or do they fit perfectly, etc? Then they draw it on their papers.

6. **What is the character's job?** – Again, list jobs on the board and have students vote. You will notice in the video I said "job" in French instead of "*travail*." For lower levels, I try to use as many cognates as possible.

7. **What kinds of accessories does the character have?** – For example, our monkey was a magician, so we gave him a magic wand and a tophat.

8. **What is the character like?** – Is the character nice? Mean? Selfish? Intelligent? Stupid? Get as many character traits as possible from the students and write them on the board, then have them vote then draw.

9. **What is the character's name?** – Write down the ideas students give you, vote, and then have the students write the character's name on the paper.

These are just suggestions; feel free to ask for input on anything you like. The sky is the limit! For lower levels, you may need to give suggestions and have students vote between two ideas; upper levels will be able to throw out more ideas on the fly.

Next, I have the students turn their papers over, and we write the story. I usually start the story for the students, and as we write, I stop on details and ask them to give me the details from the pictures they drew. I underline those details. I also add more details, for example, I ask them where the character lives, if the character has a family, etc. When writing verbs, I usually ask the students for the correct conjugation; however, first-year students may not have that information yet, so I write it for them and underline it. Then we come up with a title for the story, which often in the lower levels is just the name of the character and its job.

The last part of the activity is to have the students take each line of the story and illustrate it. Usually, I have them make a little book and turn it in. You can also have them do it on a piece of paper. I also have a template you can have them use. You can also go back to past stories (hence the reason why I like to save them on the big Post-it papers) and have them create a book. An extension might be to take a past story and create a "Mad Lib"-type fill-in-the-blank activity and have them write their own stories.

Bringing the World into Your Classroom

I would like to start this chapter with the following quotes from Freida Pinto, George Santayana, and Hugh Cevans because they speak to the content of the chapter: "There's so much happening around the world and the only way to be more well versed is to be a GLOBAL CITIZEN traveling from one place to another all the time." – Freida Pinto; "A man's feet should be planted in his country but his eyes should survey the world." – George Santayana; "When you make global citizenship your mission, you suddenly find yourself with extraordinary allies." – Hugh Cevans.

I chose these quotes to begin the chapter because I feel that travel and connecting with other people and cultures is essential to a person's education. Travel is also a privilege. As language teachers, we often can travel with our students, but we also must understand that these types of opportunities are not equitable. For this reason, learning to bring the world into our classrooms in a way that every student can benefit is crucial.

I love to travel. Every time I travel to a new place, I see it as a chance to bring my experiences in the world back to my students. In the last few years since COVID, it has become abundantly clear to me how important human connection is to the fabric of society. Undesirable behaviors from grown adults have increased exponentially as has divisiveness and outright hatred for the "other." With all this turmoil, educators are becoming so burnt out and mentally exhausted that they walk out of their classrooms in droves and never look back because they are just tired. They are tired of parents throwing tantrums. They are tired of being blamed for all that is wrong in the world and tired of giving so much that they have nothing left to give.

Eight per cent of teachers leave the profession every year, and nearly 50% leave the profession within the first five years. The number one reason teachers leave the profession is increasing professional demands with decreasing support. Support doesn't just refer to salary, although teachers are asked to do more work, and their compensation doesn't necessarily increase accordingly. Support refers to an overall lack of support from parents and administrators, a lack of respect from the community, and a significant lack of training and professional development. In our changing world, many teachers have expressed not feeling equipped or supported in providing what is needed for students to thrive in the 21st century! Teachers feel frustrated because the mindset of education by influential stakeholders remains antiquated, and teachers are not treated as the professionals they are!

When teachers travel, experience the world, and interact with others who are different than themselves, they can bring those experiences back into the classroom. In October 2021, while on a work trip to Dakar, I was interviewed on a show called *The Talk* which airs on the PanAfrican News Station *Label Télévision*. During the interview, the journalist interviewing me, Georges Aboke, asked why I choose to concentrate my immersion and travel programs on teachers instead of students. It's true. In the past, I have worked exclusively with students.

When I opened my online language school in 2016, my goal was to get as many K-12 students as possible to learn languages. Up until this past year, when I traveled with groups, it was always with groups of middle and high school students. Like everyone, when COVID hit, I reflected on what I wanted to do and how I wanted to do it. For those who didn't realize it before, COVID made it abundantly clear how essential teachers are in the lives of children.

Further, the experiences of our teachers directly affect the experiences of the students in their classrooms. Teachers are in a prime position to open, excite, motivate, and engage students through their own experiences. Teachers are at the forefront of ensuring our students gain the skills they need to thrive in the 21st century real world. I have identified three essential things that teachers need to bring the real world into their classrooms effectively. Maybe you can think of more, and if you do, please comment with them! These are the three I have identified:

1 **Advocates** – Every teacher needs people in their corner who genuinely believe in them, what they are doing, and how they

are doing it. Teachers need to know that they are trusted to be the professionals they studied so long to become. Teachers need to know that parents, administrators, and community members are on their side and will go to bat for them when needed.

2. **Opportunities** – Teachers need opportunities and time for their own professional learning and collaboration. The number one complaint I hear from teachers is that their administrators don't have enough time to support them. The second complaint I often hear is that teachers are not given enough collaborative or professional learning time. Additionally, when I speak to pre-service teachers or new teachers, I often hear how they do not feel prepared to teach the populations they serve. Teacher preparation programs should have more opportunities for teaching underrepresented student populations.

3. **Resources** – Teachers need to be given the tools to do their jobs effectively. Many teachers are handed a book and told, "teach this" without formal training on using the materials. While teachers are excellent at "making lemons out of lemonade," in many cases, teachers need the opportunity to ask questions about the resources they are given. Further, they need to have a voice in the resources they use and how they use those resources. Often, standards get changed to fit an agenda for standardized testing, and teachers are just expected to teach a new way without any training! That is not ok. Further, how can we expect teachers to teach 21st-century skills and be more culturally responsive with a 20th-century toolkit? It just doesn't work!

The bottom line is that we need to support our teachers by giving them opportunities and resources to bring back into the classroom. In the interview, I made it clear that student involvement in our programs is essential. Still, it is also secondary to the work we need to do to support our teachers and give them a useable 21st-century toolkit so that students can thrive.

A 21st-century toolkit includes:

- Experiences that illuminate all of our senses
- Ongoing training in new ideas and ways of helping students access information

- Ongoing training on the neuroscience of learning
- Resources that connect the experiential learning to what will happen in the classroom
- A support person who will be with the teacher during the learning process and lots of time for collaboration
- Lesson and unit plan that teachers can use immediately to share their experiences with their students.
- Ongoing training for building relationships with students and supporting social-emotional learning.

I heard a quote recently that stuck with me: "You can't change the world if you cannot change your perception of it." As teachers, it is our job to help our students learn to think critically and change their perceptions and challenge their implicit biases. I have said over and over again that we cannot ask our students to do this if we do not do it ourselves. Part of doing the work ourselves is changing and challenging our perceptions. We cannot change the world unless we change our perception of it, and we cannot change our perception of the world if we cannot see it.

Application in the Classroom

Country Studies

Each time I travel, I write a country study upon my return. Country studies are a great way to teach all four competencies, plus ensure students have a knowledge of basic geography. I emphasize map talks within the country study because I cannot tell you how many people I have met who believe that Africa is a country instead of a continent full of many countries and rich cultures. Further, a few weeks ago, I was in classrooms and had a high school student ask me if Spain was in Italy. Another student told me she had been to Oregon when I asked the class if anyone had traveled outside North America before. Therefore, Geography is an important component.

The CI Country Study lesson begins with a short geography lesson and a class writing exercise. To start the lesson, we learn the difference between a country, a continent, and a city. Then, we name examples of continents, countries within those continents, and then cities in those countries. With the geography lesson part of this activity, you can get very detailed and add more landmarks like lakes, oceans, mountain ranges, rivers, etc.

Next, we label the country we are studying on a map of the continent, the countries surrounding it, and any landmarks present on or around the continent. Again, you can keep this simple or add as much detail as you want.

After we have worked on the continent map, we move to the map of the country itself and label cities, borders, and other geographical landmarks. I also like to do a short discussion on the country's flag. Finally, once we have talked through the maps and labeled them, we write a class paragraph about the country. The students then take the section and split it up and illustrate each line to show understanding.

Kevin

Kevin is a garden gnome that travels around the world with me. In my classes, he is our official mascot. My students love Kevin because he features prominently in helping me bring the world into my classroom. I use pictures of Kevin from my travels as starters for picture talks and stories. Before I had Kevin, I had a teddy bear that a student gave me. At the time the Stephen Colbert show was popular with my third-year juniors and seniors, so they named him "Colbear." I really don't know what happened to Colbear, I lost him in one of my many moves, but then, a colleague gave me the set of gnomes because she had seen the movie *Le Fabuleux Destin d'Amélie Poulin* (just *Amélie* in English). In the movie,

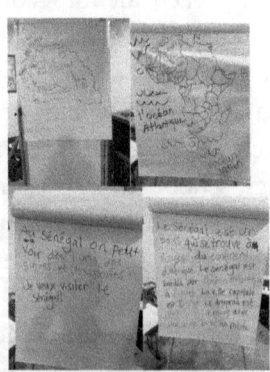

Figure 8.1 Map Talk Samples

LE SÉNÉGAL

FICHE PÉDAGOGIQUE

This is a Language with the Five Senses Education (LW5S Ed) Comprehensible Input (CI) lesson. LW5S CI is different from traditional CI in that it is a zero-translation method. Zero-translation means that English is not used to give students meaning. Instead, we use cognates, context, gestures, and images. For a video demonstration of this lesson, scan the QR code or visit this link - https://www.lw5seducation.com/post/ci-country-study-senegal

Before beginning, I go over the rules of these activities with the students:
1. **No translating from French to English.** That means the students cannot repeat what I say to them in French back to me in English. Lower levels can give me ideas in English or answer my questions in English and I will repeat what they said back to them in French usually.
2. **Everyone participates**- The picture dictionary is there so students who are quieter can hold up the picture if they choose. Everyone must vote when given choices, everyone must be paying attention and following along which includes copying the story down.
3. **If you don't know a word for something you can:**
   a. draw it
   b. act it out
   c. describe it
      i. This is meant to discourage students from defaulting to English.
4. **Do not write anything until I say "écrivez!" or draw anything until I say "dessinez"**- We have to make final decisions on the story before we write anything and I don't want students drawing on the maps or flags until we have finished discussing.

The lesson starts with some information about Senegal. I copy the blank maps onto large pieces of easel paper, but you can also project them on the board or use a smartboard. I like the low-tech solution because I love drawing and coloring with markers.
The students get blank copies of the maps from this packet.

The pages that say "clé" on them are for you to use as a guide for ideas. Sometimes I project the clé pages of North America to show a comparison between Africa and North America, asking questions like:
- Combien de chaînes de montagnes y-a-t-il en afrique? Combien en Amérique?
- Le Sénégal est un petit pays ou un grand pays? Donnez un example d'un autre petit pays.
- Les États-Unis est un grand pays ou un petit pays? Donnez un exemple d'un autre grand pays.

I go over the continent first, locating Senegal on the continent and we choose a color to color it in on the map. We label the countries around Senegal and some of the geography.
Then I go over the map of Senegal and we mark the major cities, any geographical landmarks, the ocean, etc. I ask the students questions all the way through.

I will often ask students in lower levels yes or no questions, or give them two or three choices and have them vote. As they progress through the proficiency levels, the questions become more open-ended and I ask for more detailed output from them.

The picture dictionary is meant to help students find ideas but it is also for you, as the teacher, to find ideas to draw from. You will most likely introduce a tremendous amount of vocabulary through this activity and as you do so, make sure you are drawing and labeling it so the students can copy it. There are blank picture dictionary pages so they can add more words and drawings to their repertoire.

Figure 8.2 Senegal Country Study

a flight attendant "borrows" a garden gnome from Amelie's father and takes the gnome around the world with her, snapping pictures along the way. She then secretly returns the gnome to its owner along with an album of photos. The idea of a roaming gnome didn't just come from *Le Fabuleux Destin d'Amélie Poulin*; however, roaming gnomes have been around forever! The travel site *Travelocity* had a roaming gnome in all

Book Resources QR Code

Figure 8.3 Kevin the Class Mascot

of its advertising for years. The concept actually dates back to the 1980s when the prank of stealing garden gnomes and taking them random places and snapping pictures began. There's actually a term for this; it's called *gnoming*. Kevin got his name because I felt Kevin was a funny name for a gnome and my students agreed!

If you travel as much as I do, I highly suggest getting your own version of Kevin. I guarantee your students will love it, even the middle and high schoolers and especially if your gnome is as silly as Kevin! My eigth, ninth, and tenth graders love Kevin! In fact, my own children have really embraced traveling with Kevin, and they *love* to conspire with him! They are all too willing to get Kevin into some lighthearted trouble!

Introducing cultures and experiences through the adventures of a roaming gnome has been only one of my strategies for bringing the world to my students. Over the years, I have become increasingly focused on cultivating a population of globally minded and globally competent world citizens. *Global mindedness* requires these exercises that explore what it means to be a global citizen; however, it goes beyond those initial lessons. It has to be a major mindset and part of the culture in your classroom in order to really be effective. As teachers, we have to be very intentional in every part of our teaching to ensure that our students develop a global competency. *Global competence* refers to the ability of individual students to understand the world in which they live and *their role in it*. It also extends to a willingness to address global issues and actively be the change in the world. A classroom that is *globally competent* is one where students are challenged daily to connect with and serve others, interact with kindness, and seek to understand situations and viewpoints they do not understand.

Even if you are a teacher who is not able to travel as much as I do, you can still make use of a classroom mascot such as Kevin! Here are some ideas:

- Take your mascot wherever you go and take pictures of it there – the grocery store, to sporting events, out to dinner, wherever you go! Create stories or picture talks about what your mascot was doing in those places.
- Send your mascot home overnight with individual students and ask students to take or draw pictures of all the activities they did with the mascot. Ask the students to write a story about their experiences with the mascot or talk about their experiences the next day.
- Create a travel experience for the mascot where you pose it in pictures you draw or find on the internet. Create a guided writing or a story about the mascot's trip. Ask the students to create their own travel experience. You can even use Google Earth!

It is a learning environment where students are encouraged to respect and value other cultures, people, and viewpoints, knowing that different perspectives offer a great deal of richness. It is an environment where students and teachers embrace diversity. Further, a globally competent classroom is one that teaches *decolonized curriculum* that represents all students. *Decolonized curriculum* refers to rethinking, reframing, and reconstructing curricula that favor the White and European "Colonial" lens to include all cultures and knowledge systems in the curriculum. The truth is that students today *need* to be globally competent in order to not only survive but thrive in our increasingly diverse and interconnected world!

I have several suggestions for creating a globally competent classroom:

1. **Service learning** – Service learning is a great way to bring awareness of issues in your own community, as well as global issues to the attention of your students, and create meaningful opportunities for language practice. Service learning projects create opportunities for students to serve others while finding workable solutions to global issues at the local level. Service learning is an excellent way to help students connect with others and understand how they can make a difference. There are several different ways to facilitate service learning in the world language classroom. Some ideas for service learning include:

    - Having older students visit elementary classrooms and teach the target language to younger children.
    - Have the students use the United Nations Educational, Scientific, and Cultural Organization's (UNESCO) Sustainable Development Goals (SDGs) to research global issues in a country of interest and create a service project around one of the 17 SDGs. For example, the eighth graders in my school created a beach cleanup project here in Dakar during a unit on respecting the environment based on SDGs 14 and 15 Life on Land and Life on Water (www.sdgs.un.org).
    - Integrate small acts of service into international travel programs. I often bring teachers and groups of students to Senegal. When I do this, we have several schools here in Dakar and Saint Louis that are in need of school supplies. As part of the travel program, we deliver school supplies to these schools.
    - Create poster or power point campaigns to bring awareness to and issues in a country where your target language is spoken. Students can go beyond this by thinking through solutions and real ways they can help.

2. **Virtually travel the world** – When I was a classroom teacher, I was determined to find ways to focus on the Francophone

countries that were not European. Many don't realize that French is spoken on five continents, and the majority of French speakers in the world are from Africa. In fact, French is on track to become the most spoken language in the world by the year 2050 specifically due to the increasing number of French speakers on the African continent. One year, I chose nine Francophone countries, one for each month, and designed my curriculum around these countries. This was in the early years of Google Earth. Each lesson for an entire month was focused around the country and the culture. We did a nine-month-long tour of La Francophonie. I found stories from that country; we watched videos, studied news stories, made art projects, cooked food, and went site seeing! At the time, streaming wasn't easy, but I had a subscription to TV5 Monde (the worldwide French language channel) on my cable and would record shows, newscasts, and clips to show my students in class. Now TV5 Monde is online, and I can pull videos from any French-speaking country to use. There are similar international TV stations such as Al Jazeera and Telemundo, which are in multiple languages such as Arabic, Spanish, and French. I found people who lived in our community from those countries to visit class! Today it's even easier because we can bring anyone from virtually anywhere into the classroom through the magic of Zoom! Of course, Colbear was always along with us! As I traveled around the world and visited those countries, I was able to bring my experiences into our simulations, enriching the connections for the students. They absolutely loved it and they learned *so much*. The fun part of this is using countries I have visited, but get the students' input too! Maybe there is a country they would really like to visit and study! I have a colleague in England who does all sorts of virtual tours with her students; she even has tour guides in those countries who show her students around! It's incredible! I've actually been known to do this too; when I am traveling, I let my students know to be online at a certain time and take them on a virtual tour! I've also asked friends to get on Zoom with my students and show them around. Technology has made so much possible!

3. **Classroom exchange** – The teacher colleague I mentioned in England has also established virtual partnerships with teachers in other countries. Their students connect regularly via video call and interact. This is an excellent way that you can use technology to connect students with others their own age around the world! Amity International has a really cool cultural exchange program for classrooms!

4. **Create a time during your week that is dedicated to current events and global issues** – Bring a focus to current events and global issues by creating regular opportunities for students to learn about, discuss, and create solutions. Every Friday in French class, we would watch a news story from TV5 Monde, or we'd read an article from a French newspaper. When studying current events, it's very important to encourage students to process their own thoughts and feelings, but then think about the issue from another perspective. It's also important to give the students and opportunity to come up with viable solutions to the problem and how they can actively make a difference. It is also important that these opportunities are integrated across content areas.

These are just a few in a long list of ideas and strategies for bringing the world into your classroom and to your students. My biggest piece of advice though is that *you yourself* have to get out there in the world and experience it. As teachers, we *must* experience the world in order to authentically bring it to the kids who cross our thresholds every single day. It is never too late to start your own journey to global competence!

Bringing the World into the Classroom Through Food

I don't know a language teacher out there who doesn't use food in some capacity in the classroom. Food is always a direct link to culture and an easy way to introduce cultural experiences to students. Every culture in the world has certain traditional dishes and customs around food. As a high school French teacher, we often made crêpes, ratatouille, croissants, and Croque Messiurs, and had cheese tastings. As I have evolved in my teaching and continued to decolonize my curriculum, I have added food experiences from Francophone Africa such as thieboudienne, mafé, and yassa. Spanish teachers in the United States have ample opportunity and resources for sharing Mexican food, but the Spanish speaking world has such rich recipes as arepas, paella, papusas, and empanadas. A Chinese teacher in my school also made dumplings with her students for Chinese New Year!

For years I did a project with my first years called Café Day where students had to create their own cafés, and we would invite the community and others in the school to eat in our cafés. Pictured below is the last café day that I was a classroom French teacher. Café Day was always a lot of work but an incredibly popular project, and the students learned *so much* about French café culture! Most importantly, they were applying the skills they learned in the classroom to a situation they could encounter in real life. This project was successful on so many levels.

Café Day was always the highlight of the year for me, my students, and those who participated. The project's premise is simple – the unit on Le Café et Le Restaurant always came at the very end of the school

Figure 8.4 Café Day Pictures

year in first-year French. The final project of the year, the summative assessment for the entire year, and the last unit were for the students to create their own French cafés. They planned, organized, and executed a real café with real food!

We invited French speakers living in the community and students' families, and other school community members to be our customers. The last year I was able to do this project in person. We even had the news media visit our classroom! I had a tiny class of six students, all girls, so we made one café instead of multiple and held it in my classroom. The school was tiny, with no more than 50 students in the whole school in grades K-12. It was amazing because I had a kitchen attached to my classroom to do all the cooking and preparations. It was enjoyable to watch them and interact with everyone who attended. The icing on the cake was that this project I had been doing for years was highlighted on the evening news! When I was no longer in the classroom and working as an administrator, I really missed Café Day, and I still do.

The Café Day project was so much more than the application of linguistic and cultural skills though. It was teamwork, cooperative learning skills, critical thinking, following directions, and planning. This project helped students develop skills they would need for their whole lives, and that is why I include cooking in many of my thematic units.

In every country study I write, I include four recipes from that culture. When children try new and different types of foods, they move outside their comfort zones, which ultimately develops the brain's prefrontal cortex. Everything I do in education is done intentionally to build those connections in the brain and further develop those executive functioning skills that are housed in the frontal lobe of the brain.

Giving students opportunities to share a meal allows them to learn table manners, bond, and facilitate conversations between students. A few years ago, I was coaching a teacher who decided to work with the cafeteria to create a formal luncheon for her students. The students had to dress nicely, sit together, talk with each other, and share the meal. I don't remember what was served, but the students were very engaged, and all tried the meal! I told this teacher that I loved this idea and encouraged her to allow more opportunities of this nature where students of diverse backgrounds could bring something special they eat in their families to school to share with their classmates.

In the school mentioned above, all food brought to school has to be prepackaged due to allergies. Prepackaged food requirements are becoming more and more common. However, sometimes teachers can get around this by cooking with their students, so I suggested that the teacher have the students bring in the recipe and cook together. The teacher was able to do this and, in the class, was able to learn all about the different cultures represented in their classroom that year! Another suggestion for getting around the "prepackaged food" requirements is to send home permission forms that parents sign.

Not only does cooking culturally validate students, but it also builds their prefrontal cortex, giving them skills they can use their entire lives. I can tell you that many of my generation never learned to cook which I find very sad. I feel so lucky that I learned to cook and that I can use that gift to share wonderful lessons with my own children and my students. Cooking is culture; it's human connection; it's love.

The Café Day project has been adapted to other language classes in the following ways by fellow colleagues:

- Arabic – tagine competition
- Spanish – Tapas restaurant
- Chinese – Chinese New Year celebration with dumpling making
- Japanese – Iron Chef competition

Virtual Trips with Google Earth

Google Earth is a great way to introduce students to different parts of the world and other cultures. I love using Google Earth to explore different countries and learn about the people who live in those countries. Google Earth is also a great way to learn about landmarks and important historical sites. For example, it is effortless to visit any UNESCO heritage sites and cities on Google Earth! I also like Google Earth for visiting the different Indigenous lands around the United States, Canada, and the world!

When creating a Google Earth lesson, I start by having students create a passport. There are several passport templates available if you Google "printable passport template" or you can use this one:

Figure 8.5 Café Day Project

Book Resources QR Code

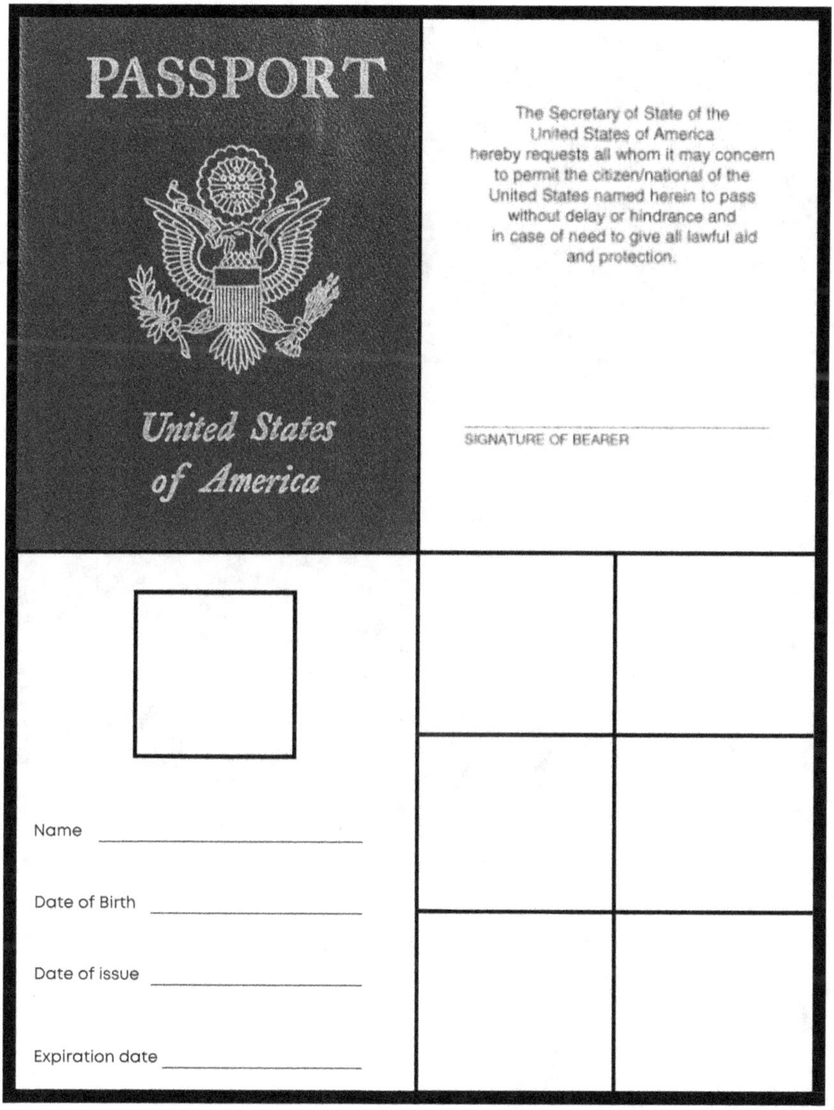

Figure 8.6 Sample Passport

Students also get a stamp in their passport and a boarding pass. Passport stamps can be found by Googling the name of the country and "passport stamp."

Here is an example of a virtual trip to Morocco:

Bringing the World into Your Classroom

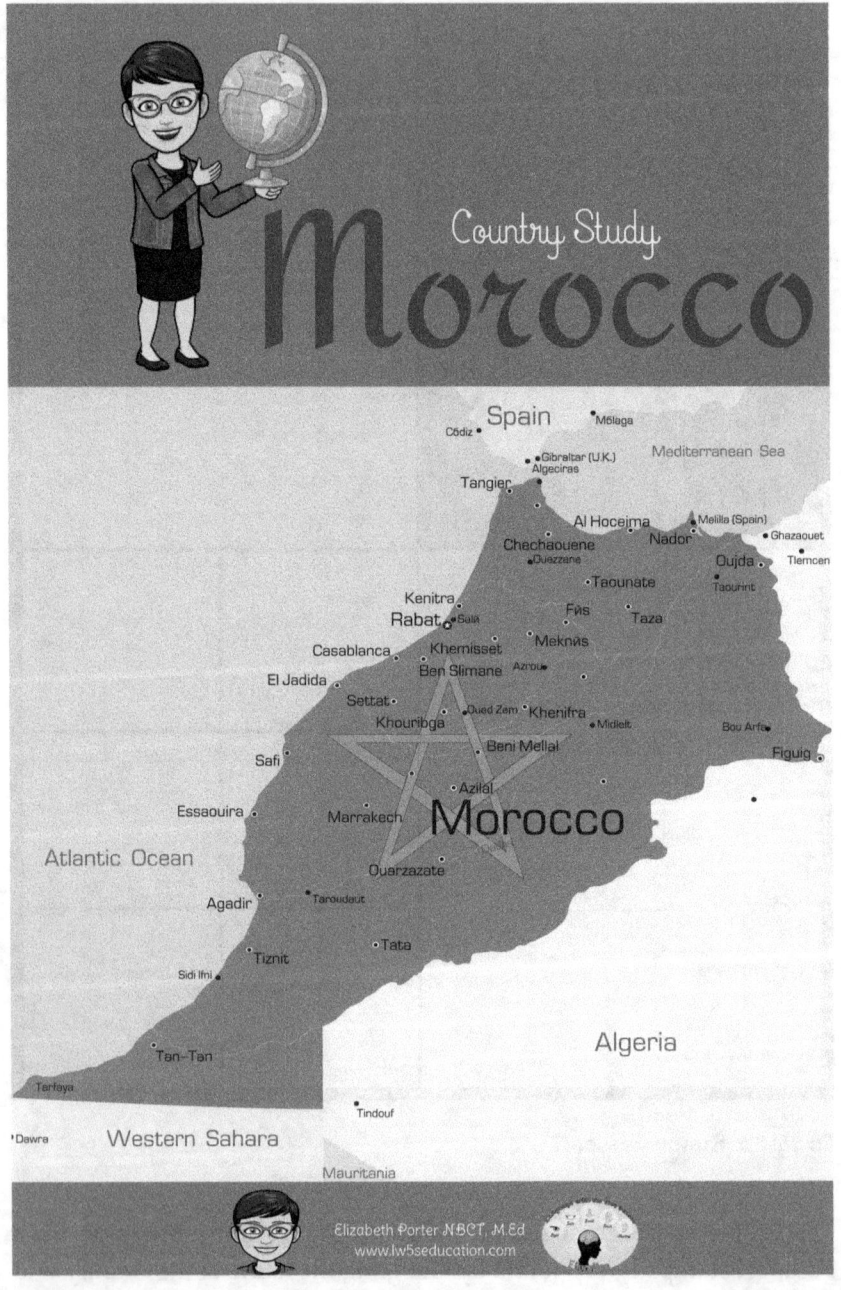

Figure 8.7 Morocco Country Study

Book Resources QR Code

Creativity in the World Language Classroom

I would like to start this chapter with the following quotes from Sir Ken Robinson, Albert Einstein, and Pablo Picasso because they speak to the content of the chapter: "Creativity is now as important in education as literacy and we should treat it with the same status." – Sir Ken Robinson; "It is the supreme art of the teacher to awaken joy in creative expression and knowledge." – Albert Einstein; "Learn the rules like a pro so you can break them like an artist." – Pablo Picasso.

These quotes introduce us to a 21st-century skill that is often overlooked – creativity. It is often believed that creativity is innate and that you are either a creative person or not. In fact, creativity is a skill that is cultivated in each person and allows for students to use new language skills in ways that are innovative. Creativity allows students to break down barriers and use language in a way that helps them be understood rather than focusing on accuracy.

Early in my teaching career, I was teaching in the era of No Child Left Behind (NCLB). At the time, in Washington State, all students had to pass the state testing at their grade level, no matter what zero exceptions. This meant that English language learners and students with learning or intellectual disabilities had a great disadvantage. I happened to be teaching in a school that was the magnet school for special education in our district. Because of this, a large number of our student population qualified on Individual Education Plans and were not able to successfully pass the state test at their grade level. My school, therefore, was labeled a "failing school" under NCLB and lost federal funding. The first programs to be cut were arts, French, and Japanese in order to dedicate more money to remedial math and English classes.

Unfortunately, cutting arts and language classes is a huge detriment to students, especially those who do not fit into the "standardized testing" box. I have always said, "we don't have standardized kids, so why do we standardized test?" I once had a student who told me that my class was the only reason she came to school. That statement is powerful because in many cases, the classes that are considered "electives" are the reason why many students get up in the morning and come to school every day. Language and arts classes are safe havens for many students, where they can shine and feel comfortable expressing their authentic selves.

Bilingualism and creativity are two of the essential 21st-century skills that build executive functioning skills in the prefrontal cortex of the brain and work in harmony to enhance the other 21st-century skills. People who speak more than one language can access a larger surface area of the brain, leading to enhanced and stronger neuropathways (Porter, 2019). Further, language is processed in the brain in very similar ways to music, and when language and learning is paired with movement and rhythm or music, the learner is more likely to strengthen neuropathways that embed skills in the brain. Further, music, rhythm, and body movement are associated with increased fluency because of the sensory input sent through the reticular activating system through the amygdala and directly into the prefrontal cortex.

Studies of bilinguals versus monolinguals have shown that bilinguals predominantly outperform monolinguals on creativity tasks due to their enhanced executive functioning skills in the prefrontal cortex. Further, bilinguals tend to have more experience with multiple cultures and intercultural communication than monolinguals. Enhanced creativity can be correlated to enhanced ability to innovate and problem solve by seeking out of the box solutions.

According to Sir Ken Robinson in his 2007 TED Talk *Skills Kill Creativity*, creativity is as important in education as literacy, and we need to treat it with the same status. Further, creativity is essential in language acquisition because the learner needs to be able to use the language skills in new and innovative ways, essentially creating new ideas from the new language. Creativity is enhanced by a rich vocabulary which is, in turn, enhanced by language acquisition (Morar et al., 2020).

Unfortunately, skills such as creativity and bilingualism are stifled by poor education policy that prioritizes quantitative measures that dehumanize education and privilege. Quantitative, standardized education is harmful to an equitable and quality education. These policies are meant to level the playing field with the argument that racism and diversity no longer plays a factor in a person's social position. Unfortunately, approaches such as standardized testing reinforce inequities because they require students of diverse backgrounds to be held to a "normalized white standard" and takes away from courses that foster creativity and 21st-century skills. (Stewart & Haynes, 2015).

Measurements and policies that favor standardized testing and that are solely quantitative and restrictive reflect educational disparities. Especially when only using limited quantitative data to make decisions, without taking inequities in the K-12 education system into consideration that affect a disproportionate population of students of diverse linguistic, racial, socioeconomic, and cultural backgrounds. Our children are not numbers. They need creativity to foster the essential skills needed to thrive in a 21st-century real world.

Standardization and quantitative measures in education create a reliance on literacy and numeracy. When students are not meeting standards in math and reading on high-stakes assessments, schools lose essential federal funding. Loss of federal funding means that schools will cut programs such as music, drama, and foreign language, and boost remedial math classes to raise test scores. Unfortunately, it has been proven repeatedly over multiple years that increasing math courses and decreasing arts and languages lowers test scores rather than increases them (Porter, 2020). Standardized testing is more a predictor of affluence than of academic achievement. Further, 21st-century skills go beyond literacy and numeracy.

Elimination of arts and language programs further widens the achievement gap because students who already struggle with standardization often do not have the means to participate in arts or language classes outside of school. These types of programs in an extracurricular setting are often expensive and therefore out of reach for many students. Programs that promote the arts and languages are essential for building executive functioning skills that are a vital part of a 21st-century education.

Combining language acquisition with the arts not only fosters an environment of creativity but allows students who do not fit inside the proverbial "box" to learn differently and thrive. Using the arts and creative expression is a natural part of the language acquisition process because it solidifies the connections in the brain by using the same neuropathways created to learn our native language. Creative expression in the language classroom promotes the following 21st-century skills:

- Communication in two languages
- Fluency and expression
- Critical thinking
- Problem-solving
- Teamwork
- Time management
- Leadership
- Organization
- Confidence
- Creativity

Application in the Classroom

There are many ways creativity can be promoted in the classroom through both visual and performing arts. I love to use music and rhythm because any time information is put to music or rhythm; it goes directly into the long-term memory. Further, dancing or body movements in conjunction with music and rhythm further strengthen those neuropathways.

The human brain is divided into two hemispheres. In the past, it has been thought that a person is either right-brain dominant or left-brain dominant. Right-brain-dominant people have typically been considered more creative, innovative, emotional, and subjective. On the other hand, left-brain-dominant people have traditionally been considered more analytical, logical, orderly, and better at math and science. However, in recent years, studies have shown that the brain's two hemispheres work together, and the learning environment and the way learners receive information in the brain and apply that learning is more indicative of a person's creativity and innovation (Kim et al., 2022).

Learner-centered approaches that integrate language acquisition with creativity allow the students to be active participants in their learning. We are no longer in an era where students are empty receptacles filled with knowledge by the teacher who knows all. The only way to ensure that learners are ready for the 21st-century real world is to ensure that all students have access to programs that build executive functioning skills through creative and innovative processes. We can do this by integrating activities in the classroom that promote creativity.

In every lesson and thematic unit, I like to offer multiple ways to assess the application of knowledge and skills. One of my favorite ways to promote creativity and differentiate for students is to offer what I call *"tic tac tableau au choix"* or "Tic Tac Choices." Students have to pick three assessment activities in a row to show they have acquired and can apply the skills learned during the unit.

Some choices include:

- **Puppet shows** – Puppet shows are great because not every student wants to be in the spotlight. A puppet show allows students to be creative without being put on the spot.
- **Comic strip or comic book story** – I love comics because it allows students who enjoy drawing to express themselves through drawing. Comics are also easy to read and can be adapted to any proficiency level.
- **Scavenger hunts** – I love to give students the opportunity to get out of the classroom, and scavenger hunts are a great way for students to express themselves creatively while using the language skills they are learning. To take this a step further, students can design scavenger hunts for each other! Some of the most fun and creative scavenger hunts have been designed by students in my classes! They love this activity because it allows them to put their own personalities and creativity into the activity.
- **Children's books** – One activity students love is when I ask them to create a children's book out of a story that we created in class. I will often give this assignment in groups and have each group contribute pages to one class book. The students get creative with these books. Other times, I compile our class stories into a book from the school

year and each student gets a copy! This is an excellent way to show students their progress from the beginning to the end of the year!

- **Bilingual theater** – This is a special activity that I designed with the Senegalese actor Ibrahima Mbaye (the choice board below is based on a classroom interview activity with Ibrahima). Bilingual theater is an activity where we choose a story in the target language, and the students put on a play based on the story. The students create the script, the costumes, the sets, and all that goes into putting on a play. The students then perform the story for other students and their families, and we have even gone into elementary classrooms to perform for younger children. The students love this activity, and it gives them a sense of ownership over their linguistic abilities. Not only that, but it involves students who may not want to be the "actors" because they help with other parts of the production.

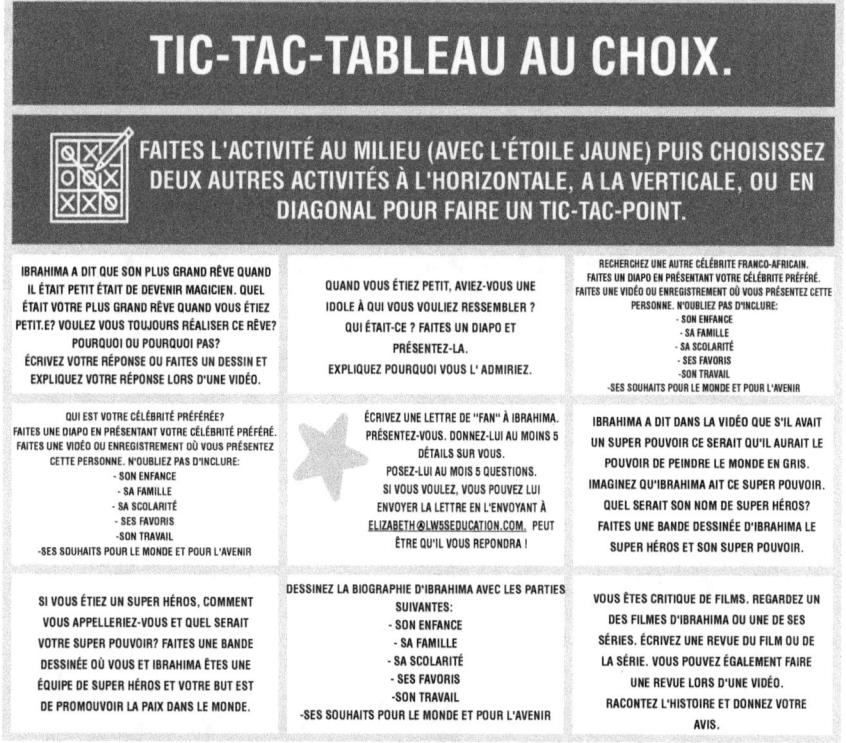

Figure 9.1 Sample Choice Board for Assessment

- *Cacaphonie* – *Cacaphonie* is a word in French that is used to mean "imitation of sounds." I like to use this as a sort of brain break for students, but it also allows them to use creativity because they interpret the sound themselves. For example, I may tell them to make certain animal sounds, sound like a Harley Davidson motorcycle, make a sound like a car horn, sound like a train, and sound like an ambulance. This activity can go a little further by asking students to add body movements to the sounds.

Bibliography

Bialystok, E., Luk, G., & Kwan, E. (2005). Bilingualism, biliteracy, and learning to read: Interactions among languages and writing systems. *Scientific Studies of Reading, 9*(1), 43–61. https://doi.org/10.1207/s1532799xssr0901_4

Crozier, G. (2015). Middle-class privilege and education. *British Journal of Sociology of Education, 36*(7), 1115–1123. https://doi.org/10.1080/01425692.2015.1076249

Davies, P. (1990, January 1). *[PDF] the use of drama in English language teaching: Semantic scholar*. undefined. Retrieved March 8, 2022, from https://www.semanticscholar.org/paper/The-Use-of-Drama-in-English-Language-Teaching-Davies/8bfbe4064cea5e74323aba2cfee5ba3fb769bc9a

Dijk, M., Kroesbergen, E. H., Blom, E., & Leseman, P. P. (2018). Bilingualism and creativity: Towards a situated cognition approach. *The Journal of Creative Behavior, 53*(2), 178–188. https://doi.org/10.1002/jocb.238

Do schools kill creativity? (2007). *YouTube*. Retrieved March 8, 2022, from https://youtu.be/iG9CE55wbtY

Flores, N. (2016, July 18). *Bilingualism is a 21st century skill. So why are 21st century standards ignoring it?* C-SAIL. Retrieved March 8, 2022, from https://www.c-sail.org/resources/blog/bilingualism-21st-century-skill-so-why-are-21st-century-standards-ignoring-it

Gelitz, C. (2021, November 12). *How certain gestures help you learn new words*. Scientific American. Retrieved September 15, 2022, from https://www.scientificamerican.com/article/how-certain-gestures-help-you-learn-new-words/

Bibliography

Grabmeier, J. (2019, April 9). *The importance of reading to kids daily*. College of Education and Human Ecology. Retrieved September 16, 2022, from https://ehe.osu.edu/news/listing/importance-reading-kids-daily-0

Henriksen, D., Misra, P., & Fisser, P. (n.d.). *Infusing creativity and technology in 21st century ...* Retrieved March 9, 2022, from http://danah-henriksen.com/wp-content/uploads/2016/10/creativity-systemic-view.pdf

Henze, R. (1998). *The Urban Review*, 30(3), 187–210. https://doi.org/10.1023/a:1023280117904

Honigsfeld, A. (2019). *Growing language & literacy: Strategies for English learners: Grades K-8*. Heinemann.

Kim, S., Raza, M., & Seidman, E. (2022). *Improving 21st-century teaching skills: The key to ...* Retrieved March 9, 2022, from https://journals.sagepub.com/doi/10.1177/1745499919829214

Lewis, R. (n.d.). *What is comprehensible input and why does it matter for language learning?* Leonardo English. Retrieved October 31, 2022, from https://www.leonardoenglish.com/blog/comprehensible-input

Maranz, E. D. (2001). *African friends and money matters: Observations from Africa*. SIL International.

Morar, L.-L., Boștină-Bratu, S., & Negoescu, A. (2020). The importance of creativity in foreign language acquisition. *Land Forces Academy Review*, 25(3), 217–222. https://doi.org/10.2478/raft-2020-0026

Moule, J. (2012). *Cultural competence: A primer for educators*. Wadsworth Publishing.

Porter, E. (2020). *Performance based solution*. Petit Renard Press.

Projet des Classes Mondiales. (2021). *YouTube*. Retrieved September 28, 2022, from https://youtu.be/MgUL3BKQlvc.

Seechaliao, T. (2017). Instructional strategies to support creativity and innovation in education. *Journal of Education and Learning*, 6(4), 201. https://doi.org/10.5539/jel.v6n4p201

For Product Safety Concerns and Information please contact our EU representative GPSR@taylorandfrancis.com
Taylor & Francis Verlag GmbH, Kaufingerstraße 24, 80331 München, Germany

www.ingramcontent.com/pod-product-compliance
Lightning Source LLC
Chambersburg PA
CBHW050600300426
44112CB00013B/2011